Rev. Marian Plant
321 Maywinn Dr.
Defiance, OH 43512

hopeful REALISM

D0111222

Douglas F. Ottati

hopeful REALISM

Reclaiming the Poetry of Theology

The Pilgrim Press
Cleveland, Ohio

The Pilgrim Press, Cleveland, Ohio 44115
© 1999 by Douglas F. Ottati

Biblical quotations are from the New Revised Standard Version of the Bible, © 1989 by the Division of Christian Education of the National Council of the Churches of Christ in the U.S.A., and are used by permission

Published 1999. All rights reserved

Printed in the United States of America on acid-free paper

04 03 02 01 00 99 5 4 3 2 1

Library of Congress Cataloging-in-Publication Data
Ottati, Douglas F.
Hopeful realism : reclaiming the poetry of theology / Douglas F. Ottati.
p. cm.
Includes bibliographical references and index.
ISBN 0-8298-1322-5 (pbk. : alk. paper)
1. Theology, Doctrinal. I. Title.
BT80.O87 1999
230—ddc21 98-37473
CIP

for the

THEOLOGY DISCUSSION GROUP

Contents

Acknowledgments

The chapters of this book began as lectures at churches, colleges, seminaries, and ministers' associations. As a result, I have many people and institutions to thank as I bring this project to completion.

Lucy Forster Smith invited me to deliver what eventually became chapter 1 as a convocation address at Macalester College in St. Paul, Minnesota, in February of 1996. I am grateful to Thomas Mainor and Donald McKim for the opportunity to speak on the topic of chapter 2 at Memphis Theological Seminary in March 1998. An earlier version of chapter 3 was published in *The Christian Century* (November 8, 1995). In November 1996, the ASK class at Lexington Presbyterian Church in Lexington, Virginia, read and discussed an earlier draft of chapter 4, and I should like to thank Bill and Deb Klein for their hospitality on that occasion. David Nikkel invited me to lecture on incarnation and ecumenical theology, the topic of chapter 5, at Hastings College in Hastings, Nebraska, in October 1996, when I also enjoyed the good company of David Stipp in Ord, Nebraska. Roger Gench arranged for me to speak on this same topic to a group of ministers in Baltimore in November of 1997. In substance, chapter 6, "Engaging Culture," began as a presentation at Bunker Hill Presbyterian Church in Bunker Hill, West Virginia, in honor of John Harris's ten (very fine) years in the ministry. I delivered a subsequent version in Albuquerque, New Mexico, in June 1996 at a meeting of *Semper Reformanda,* a network of groups and persons within the Presbyterian Church (U.S.A.) who are committed to the gospel, open to new expressions, and concerned about current issues of liberation, justice, and the integrity of creation. I would like to thank Robert Stone for the opportunity to be there. Chapter 7 began as a presentation for the Ministers' Retreat of National Capital Presbytery in October 1997. In July 1997, I spoke on the topics of several of the chapters in this book in five lectures at the Conference on Interpreting the Faith at Union Theological Seminary and Presbyterian School of Christian Education. The Trustees of Union Theological Seminary in Virginia granted me sabbatical leave in 1996–1997, during which time I was able to put most of my lectures into manuscript form.

Paul E. Capetz, Martin L. Cook, Lois K. Daly, Dawn DeVries, James Calvin Davis, Cheryl Hubbard, Thomas James, Robin W. Lovin, Terence Martin, Richard B. Miller, David Roberts, Angela Romano, William Schweiker, Douglas Schuurman, Charles M. Swezey, Randy Tremba, David True, and Charles Wilson all read and commented on portions of the manuscript at various stages. Timothy G. Staveteig, my editor at The Pilgrim Press, offered his good help and encouragement. Robert Johnson helped me put the text into final form.

Thanks are also due to Dave, Donna, Gene, and Jeff at Puddn'-heads' Coffee House, where I spent enough time writing and revising to be charged rent. This is a good place to thank J. Frederick Holper, my good friend and colleague at Union, who now moves to McCormick Theological Seminary. I shall miss our regular conversations over supper on Wednesday evenings. I continue to owe special debts of gratitude to the people who put up with me on a daily basis: Pamela, Katherine, and Albert.

Finally, this book is dedicated with affection and respect to all those who have met on Friday afternoons during the past fifteen years at various establishments in Richmond, Virginia, in order to discuss theology and ethics over a good drink at a fair price.

Introduction

This book explores Christian theology as a reflective enterprise that helps us to envision God, the world, and ourselves. My explorations have been guided by three convictions.

THREE GUIDING CONVICTIONS

The first conviction is that a Christian theologian works with the church's poetry (the many symbols, images, and patterns that emerge in the church's scriptures, traditions, and contemporary life) in order to portray the world, our possibilities, and our limits in relation to God. Theology traffics in images, symbols, and themes that clarify life in its true depth and circumstance. Thus, the great doctrines of Christian theology help us to orient our lives as they point toward and put us in touch with that which remains beyond our comprehension. They do not offer detached descriptions of things completely known so much as evocative images, patterns, models, and paradigms that interpret and explore but never entirely capture the reality within which we live and move and have our being. In this sense, the language of theology operates at a different level and with a different purpose than the quantitative discourse that has come to dominate so many aspects of our culture.

This assumption puts me at odds with those who reduce theology to literal or narrowly scientific statements. A physicist argues that "'Let there be light' may . . . be understood as designating the creation of the primeval fireball—the big bang."[1] A high school class looks at the story of Noah and the flood to "see what we can verify and what we can't."[2] A fundamentalist preacher insists that Genesis, the virgin birth, the atonement, and Jesus' resurrection are all to be understood literally, that there is no contradiction between these points and "the proven facts of science," and that the theory of evolution is bestial and wrong.[3] At the other end of the spectrum, Ralph Wendell Burhoe, founding editor of *Zygon: Journal of Religion and Science* and a winner of the prestigious Templeton Prize for Progress in Religion in an Age of Science, sees modern science as "a new gift of revelation," and he identifies God with an ultimate reality characterized by evolutionary natural selection.[4]

I believe that approaches such as these suffer from a reductive literal-mindedness that fails to account adequately for God, the world, and the depth of human existence.[5] The integrity and truth of Christian theology do not reside in a literal meaning or application of its basic terms and concepts, but in a more capacious and poetic reflection.

My second conviction is that Christian theology has a practical aim. Like a pastor, it tries to help persons and communities interact with current situations and realities in a manner that is faithfully responsive to God. Christian theology is a reflective enterprise whereby Christian communities attempt to envision in relation to God the many objects, situations, and realities with which we interact—everything from our biological makeups and our families to our societies and natural environments. Of course, these objects, situations, and realities are also interpreted by other religious communities, geneticists, artists, anthropologists, novelists, philosophers, psychologists, governments, political parties, physicists, sociologists, and others. This is why the practical aim of Christian theology cannot come to rest in a narrow and isolated confession. Whenever Christian theologians attempt practically relevant and faithful interpretations of the many objects, situations, and realities with which we interact, they enter into conversations with interpretations offered by other persons and communities. They engage culture.

This conviction distinguishes my approach from the work of many narrative theologians who seem content to restate the received tradition in the hope that it will simply assimilate and absorb the world into its own narrow sphere. By contrast, I understand theology as a practical reflection that tries to extend the relevance of Christian believing by bringing other interpretations and viewpoints into dialogue with Christian convictions about God. In short, Christian theology is adequate to its practical aim only when it is broadly intelligible, and it is broadly intelligible only when its reflections are both brought to bear on and informed by other interpretations of human existence in the world.[6]

My third conviction is that, when we make use of the church's poetry in order to frame a practically relevant vision of God, world, and human existence, the result is a particular stance or posture. More specifically, interlocking symbols, such as God's sovereign reign or dominion, creation, sin, providence, and redemption, yield a particular picture of life-before-God-and-God-before-life. They support an outlook that encourages us to participate in God's world; to recognize that we are fitted for true communion with God in community with others; to acknowledge our significant but limited and dependent powers and capabilities; to expect diminishment, estrangement, conflict, fragmentation, and death; but nevertheless to look for enlargement, reconciliation, and life.

This is hopeful realism, a practical stance and attitude that challenges many sensibilities and viewpoints, and that also has implications for how we may understand the church and its ministry. Hopeful realism refuses both easy optimisms and cynical pessimisms. It suggests that we do not really know ourselves when we concentrate on our abilities apart from our limits and our faults. However, it also claims that we do not truly know ourselves when we consider our limits and our faults apart from our abilities and apart from the traces of true communion in community that we encounter in God's world.

One further point. Because the essays collected here began as lectures for a wide range of audiences, they also represent an experiment in Christian theology and some of its diverse "publics." Can theology address both church or congregation and academy at the same time? I think so. Accordingly, I have tried to avoid jargon, and, where jargon seemed unavoidable, I have tried to explain it. I have also relegated many of the more scholarly points and debates to the endnotes. But this does not mean that the text has been "dumbed down." Twenty-odd years as a seminary professor has convinced me that there are people in the church (and also alongside it) who remain dissatisfied with the simplistic texts, literalistic dogmas, and shallow spiritualities that so often pass for popular theology. I am also convinced that there are some academicians who know that genuine theology—the kind that makes actual claims about God and our lives in the world—cannot be reduced to a neutral study of religion apart from any particular piety and commitment.

These suppositions animate and inform the chapters that follow. Chapter 1 concerns a current fascination in American culture. Today, popular bookstores are filled with titles such as *The Leader in You* and *Super-Leadership,* universities are opening schools of leadership studies, and successful sports personalities offer traveling seminars with titles such as "The Competitive Edge" and "Winning at the Game of Life." I criticize "leadership-speak," as well as the narrow, manipulative, technical, and procedural sensibility of the "leader-manager" in our society that so easily joins forces with *laissez faire* and reductive social Darwinist claims that life *is* competition. I suggest that more genuine and helpful conversations about leadership will draw on an enlarged sensibility as well as a more complicated and forthrightly social picture of human life and motivation. I also suggest that a more realistic, hopeful, and humane style of leadership will envision the chief end of human life more along the lines of a common meal or banquet to which all are invited (say, a Seder or Lord's Supper), than a meticulously planned and evaluated management system.

The next four chapters present a view of theology, as well as interpretations of selected doctrines, that reject narrow sensibilities and reductive outlooks. Chapter 2 claims that Christian theology is more sacramental than technical, and that it often has as much in common with sermons, hymns, and prayers as it does with many academic monographs and treatises. I also argue that, when held together in an appropriately balanced framework, leading Christian symbols yield a hopefully realistic vision of God and ourselves that can and should be brought into conversations with other interpretations and viewpoints.

Rather than as a celestial mathematics or "an esoteric exposition of God's inner life," chapter 3 interprets the Trinity as a practical doctrine that symbolizes the relation of God to God's creatures.[7] When understood in this way, trinitarian thinking emerges from a biblically initiated exploration of redemption. It encourages us to reenvision our lives in the context of the faithful activity of the God who goes out from Godself to initiate, sustain, and renew true communion in community. It articulates a saving knowledge that lends us the confidence and the courage to participate faithfully in God's world despite the estrangements, conflicts, and anxieties that beset us.

Chapter 4 develops my sometimes controversial understanding of resurrection as a basic symbol of the Christian framework.[8] I maintain that God's raising of Jesus from the dead exalts the way of the cross, and that it lifts up Jesus Christ as the living Lord of our continuing life and experience. It indicates that the great God who creates and sustains all things is a faithful redeemer, and it intimates that the chief possibility and destiny of human life is the new and true life of God's reign. These are the chief meanings and claims of resurrection faith, and they are compatible with a relatively wide range of interpretations of what happened following Jesus' crucifixion. We therefore ought not give people the mistaken impression that they must affirm one and only one account of what happened in order to be Christian, to be saved, or to be faithful.

Again, the incarnation sometimes is presented as a conversation-stopper—a doctrine that asserts that Jesus is the only valid source of insight for Christian theology; that, in Jesus Christ, Christian theology has an exclusive purchase on truth; and that Christianity alone is true whereas all other religions are false. Chapter 5 takes a different tack by returning to the old Calvinist idea that God is truly incarnate in the finite man, Jesus of Nazareth, but that the finite man, Jesus, does not encompass, exhaust, or enclose the infinite God. I argue that contemporary theologies that are informed by this idea will be genuinely ecumenical in the sense that they will cross barriers and boundaries and so reach out to the entire inhabited world. They will resist temptations to define Christianity as true and other religions as false. They will recognize that our talk about God is symbolic talk that points toward and interprets but never entirely captures the reality of God. They will recognize that particular Christian subtraditions are indispensable but also open to continuing conversation and revision. Finally, they will appreciate the importance of different faith traditions as well as of continuing conversation among them.

The book closes with two chapters about the church, its ministry, and its mission in contemporary America. Chapter 6 claims that, in and through a somewhat traumatic devaluation of our cultural clout and authority, God is calling "mainline" Protestants in America to reflect seriously, explicitly, and creatively about the manner of their participation in the world. I argue that we should reject retreats into a new otherworldliness or a new "churchiness." Indeed, the truth of the gospel encourages us to commit ourselves anew to a faithfully participatory, hopefully realistic, and culturally engaging ministry.

Chapter 7 tries to outline this ministry. It points to a kind of leadership, to a witness that is less concerned with competition and calculation than with the great adventure of reconciliation and genuine community. It endorses a mission that fragments and falters again and again, and so stands in need of renovation and renewal again and again.

1 Leadership-Speak in Contemporary Society

Consider the belief that we are essentially selfish individuals seeking our separate advantages, and that our tireless attempts to manipulate one another constitute the prime engine for social advancement. Call this maladroit social Darwinism inherently exploitative, inhumane, or realistic. Call it the soul of Reaganomics, Thatcherism, or the Republican Revolution. Call it what you will. From the business section to sports columns to editorials, from Congress to Wall Street to Main Street, it is a large part of the temper of our time.[1]

LEADERSHIP-SPEAK

When talk about leadership relies on this rather uninspiring spirit, it becomes "leadership-speak," a rhetorical cover for the celebration of ceaseless competition. It compares successful CEOs to Wayne Gretzky and to coaches who win the Super Bowl.[2] It promises people that they can be "winners" if they register for certain seminars, listen to certain tapes, and build the skills and the confidence needed to "come out on top." Even at prestigious colleges and universities, leadership-speak amounts to a way of selling a competitive advantage. (Why send your son or daughter to Private University when it costs so much money? Because over here we're educating tomorrow's leaders. Across town at State U., not to mention Community College, they're training followers.)[3]

Leadership-speak is pernicious because it is reductive. It artificially narrows the complexity, the confusion, and the dynamism of life by insisting on a single pattern for everything. The predictable result is that politics, business, education, and virtually all else are portrayed as instruments in the obsessive game of trying to secure one's own isolated advantage against "the competition." Moreover, it is important to realize that leadership-speak itself has become a big business. Thumb through your in-flight magazine, and note the advertisements for seminars, tapes, books, and computer programs that promise to "strengthen the skills that are keys to success in business and in life."[4] Scan your local newspaper, and find notices for a session by a well-known sports commentator on "Winning at the Game of Life" that includes attention to "Slam-Dunking Your Way to Success" and "The Winning Formula for Enormous Achievement."[5] Cruise the business and self-help sections of a large trade bookstore, say a Borders or a Barnes and Noble, and ponder titles such as *The Leader in You: How to Win Friends, Influence People, and Succeed in a Changing World* and *SuperLeadership: Leading Others to Lead Themselves.*[6]

In this chapter, I shall point to some shortcomings of leadership-speak that cut to the core of contemporary American culture. I will suggest that leadership-speak is bound up with a manager model, a bad mysticism, and a bad mythology. I will also suggest that, if we are to move beyond leadership-speak and engage in more genuine conversations about alternative styles of leadership, we need to be open to better mysticisms and better mythologies.

THE LEADER-MANAGER

Americans are pragmatic. For us, leadership generally means moving things and people forward, solving problems, achieving goals, and "getting the job done." We elaborate and further define this rather abstract idea with the help of images and models drawn from different areas of life. Drawing on the military, for example, we may picture leadership in terms of the model of a general or commander. Then again, we may rely on the governmental image of a president, or the sports image of a team leader or coach. The field of possible images seems virtually unlimited.

In America today, however, a primary image comes from a corporate organizational context. A leader is a *manager,* someone who gets results within an organization, someone who deploys materials and human resources to achieve desired ends.[7] Thus, the successful football coach is a manager of players and assistants, as likely to be pictured wearing a tie and headphones as blowing a whistle in his sweats. Candidates for high office often promise to manage government as they would a successful business. At colleges and universities, deans and provosts manage planning processes as well as the enactment of the strategic goals and objectives that emerge from them. So do officers of volunteer organizations, churches, and synagogues. And, of course, everyone is striving to evaluate outcomes.

The leader-manager does not just crunch numbers and devise plans. She or he "uses people well."[8] That is, leader-managers develop their own abilities to communicate with others and to be open to what others have to say. Indeed, what some call the "new breed of leader" is someone who knows how to motivate and guide rather than merely direct, mentor rather than boss, facilitate and enable rather than flatly command. Such a leader views people as assets rather than expenses, and so sets about the task of supporting strong human relationships through good communication, modeling desired behaviors, coaching, and team building.[9] The leader-manager tries to foster a "healthy competition" that advances strategic goals and encourages both innovation and teamwork. He or she knows that people respond to recognition, praise, and rewards, but also that they compete successfully only when they find their jobs interesting rather than monotonous, repetitive, and trivial.[10]

The leader-manager is a goal setter.[11] This, too, is rooted in a judgment about corporate health. The organization suffers—it becomes less efficient, productive, and competitive—when people engage in activities that are not clearly related to corporate objectives. This is why leader-managers develop mental images of possible and desirable futures. On the basis of these images or goals, they help people set long-range objectives against which to measure performance. Of course, the organization's orienting goals themselves need to be checked and corrected if they are not to become ossified and counterproductive. Thus, a leader-manager not only must be disciplined in the pursuit of objectives but also must be flexible and open to adjustments and revisions.

It would be a mistake to think that, in all of this, leader-managers necessarily subject others to strategies and procedures to which they are unwilling to subject themselves. For one thing, the leader-manager is a part of the corporate plan, an employee with a specified role, responsible for making measurable progress toward objectives, and subject to regular evaluation. For another, the manager model may become deeply personally ingrained and internalized.

Consider Hyrum W. Smith's *The 10 Natural Laws of Time and Life Management: Proven Strategies for Increased Productivity and Inner Peace.* When Smith details how people can manage and get better control over their lives, his essential points read like a method for developing a personal strategic plan. He recommends identifying your governing values ("those things in your life that are of highest priority"), defining long-range goals that accord with your values, and then setting some specific intermediate goals that can be included in your list of daily tasks. This makes it possible "at the end of each day or the beginning of the following day . . . to measure the results."[12] And with this last step, the managerial routinization of life is complete.

For our purposes, two characteristics of the leader-manager deserve special comment. The first is a comparatively narrow sensibility. Persons and things—including oneself—are regarded as resources or means to management objectives. Despite a humane-therapeutic dimension, the leader-manager's predominant sensibility remains manipulative. In this model, leadership inhabits a world of strategic plans, decisions, and problems to be solved. The pathos of the leader-manager is that sensibility rarely travels beyond the routinized and rationalized patterns of corporate utility. Life becomes a matter of efficient surfaces without depths—offices, desks, electronic communications, exit ramps, elevators, indistinguishable airports, planned communities, and cul-de-sacs.

The second special characteristic of the leader-manager model is that it remains almost entirely technical and procedural and therefore inherently incomplete.[13] By itself, it says little or nothing about the point of leadership and the world in which leaders lead. What is the point of setting goals? Why pursue these goals, in particular? What is the master goal? In what sort of a world and in which areas of life does managing to objectives make sense, and how much sense does it make? Answers to questions such as these require something more than additional techniques for working with goals once we have them. They require some view of human possibilities and limits, some vision of the overall context for our leading-managing. But the leader-manager model does not provide this. It is an activist, achievement-oriented pattern in search of a philosophy, a wisdom, or a myth that indicates what life is about and what is truly important.

THE TEMPER OF THE AGE

Enter the social Darwinist temper of the age, stage right, with its insistence that life is competition, and its naive faith that ceaseless competition will somehow ensure progress toward the good. (Of course, precisely *why* ceaseless competition should ensure the good remains rather mysterious. A usual appeal is to increased productivity and wealth. But apart from "an invisible hand" or some other distributive mechanism, it is difficult to see why competitive production should benefit anyone other than the successful competitors. And there is also the nagging suspicion that, in the end, a life centered around ceaseless competition, increased productivity, and wealth may seem less than good, rather hollow, or even noxious. But I digress.) The temper of the age supports a *laissez faire* outlook, philosophy, or wisdom that helps many people to envision themselves and their world. In the light of this myth, the world is an environment overstuffed with individuals and groups competing for survival. The point of managing people and organizations is to best the competition. The point of leadership is to obtain a competitive advantage.

This is why "sports-talk" so often becomes a rather natural ally and ubiquitous cousin of leadership-speak. Life becomes a game, the ultimate match played against competitors. And within the compass of life as competition, the aim of the athlete, the coach, the manager, the *human being* is always the same: the aim is to *win*.[14]

Perhaps the most prominent alternative to this social Darwinist and *laissez faire* temper in America today is a popular therapeutic spirituality whose fundamental claim is that the chief end or master goal of life is personal growth.[15] This clearly might be understood in ways that undermine or even subvert the competitive leader-manager. For example, I might argue that genuine personal growth is stimulated by an openness to the haphazard and unplanned, and that we therefore should throw out the routinized plans that so tightly restrict our attention to specific goals and objectives. Very often, however, therapeutic spiritualities simply compensate people for the harsher aspects of competitive managerial life by recommending private havens from the "success treadmill" where people experience loving, trustful, and dependable relationships that bolster self-acceptance and self-esteem.

Indeed, therapeutic spiritualities frequently are developed in ways that explicitly support competitive managerial outlooks. Thus, we read that Pat Riley's successful approach to coaching and management in the National Basketball Association owes much to his discovery of M. Scott Peck's *The Road Less Traveled: A New Psychology of Love, Traditional Values, and Spiritual Growth.*[16] Diane Dreher's *The Tao of Personal Leadership* applies the venerable philosophy to management, business, and general systems theory.[17]

My personal favorite among the titles that join leadership, management, and spirituality is *Jesus CEO: Using Ancient Wisdom for Visionary Leadership,* by Laurie Beth Jones. Jones writes a series of short observations about Jesus and connects them with challenges of business management. For example, she says that Jesus spoke to "his staff" about their calling to work for something beyond themselves. She also notes that, when his staff turned against him and one member even betrayed him (an "experience common to many of us in business, in friendship, and in romance"), Jesus "was able to take the hit and keep on going." For Jones, this indicates that "leaders do not quit when they suffer a loss. They press on for the victory."[18]

In addition, Jones says that Jesus expressed himself and helped others to do the same. She claims that he was keenly aware of his resources, that he was open to people and their ideas, and that he "clearly defined his staff's work-related benefits." She introduces this last point by noting that "one of my financial planner friends stated, 'Jesus offered his staff one heck of a 401-K retirement plan.'" When the idea of Jesus as CEO came to Jones some years ago, she was struck that Jesus' "management style" combines the best of masculine and feminine "leadership styles," and that this combination can empower the "invaluable human energy and intelligence" that other management styles leave "untapped and underutilized."[19]

Jones is not the first American to find in Jesus the model for executive success. In a book published during the 1920s entitled *The Man Nobody Knows: A Discovery of the Real Jesus,* Bruce Barton noted that Jesus was especially good at choosing "men" of modest reputations and accomplishments and recognizing "hidden capacities in them." He claimed that "nowhere is there such a startling example of executive success as the way in which [Jesus'] organization was brought together."[20] Jesus "picked twelve men from the bottom ranks of business and forged them into an organization that conquered the world."[21] Indeed, Barton regarded Jesus as "the founder of modern business," a man who "thought of his life as [his Father's] *business.*"[22] The main points of "Jesus' business philosophy," wrote Barton, are "1. Whoever will be great must render great service. 2. Whoever will find himself at the top must be willing to lose himself at the bottom. 3. The big rewards come to those who travel the second, undemanded mile."[23]

A BETTER MYSTICISM

I have outlined the leader-manager model in some detail because I believe that it forms the mainstream cultural backdrop against which our conversations about new models and styles of leadership must proceed. There are other, less generally influential backdrops, such as the models of the compassionate counselor, the improvisational musician, and even the committed school teacher, but the leader-manager—informed by an essentially social Darwinist and competitive temper—predominates.

Precisely which models and styles may emerge as we search for alternatives to the leader-manager (and I believe that we ought to search for such alternatives) will depend in part on the qualities of our conversations and reflections. My aim here, then, is simply to suggest that, unlike reductive leadership-speak, truly interesting conversations about leadership will enlist a broader sensibility and a better mythology than those associated with the competitive leader-manager.

Interesting conversations will be informed by the conviction that the point of leadership remains obscure unless and until we gain some sense of the fullness of life and the world. We need to be carried out from ourselves to find that we alone are not the measure of reality and value. We need to discover that we are participants in a world beyond ourselves.[24] That is, interesting conversations about leadership will draw on a felt sense of interconnectedness. They will suggest the importance of apprehending others as one's fellow passengers in life and in death rather than as alien beings. They will keep faith with suffering. They will point toward a proper attentiveness to the depths of life as well as to its surfaces.

Let us call this broader, more penetrating attentiveness the mysticism without which people become less than truly humane. Let us call it the sensibility without which passion falters and leadership degenerates into a merely technical manipulation of persons and things and world. What I have in mind here is something like the live and imaginative sense of his own mortality and humanity that Scrooge owes to his haunted dreams in Charles Dickens's *A Christmas Carol.* The philosopher Cora Diamond points out that Dickens's Scrooge does not move simply and directly from a miserly and selfish spirit to a felt solidarity with others. He does not respond to mere exhortations. "He will not be able to respond to the sufferings of the Crachits until he comes to have, in his perception of their lives and their fate, a full imaginative sense of his own mortality, until he can live in the present and acknowledge his own past."[25]

In short, the enlarging of Scrooge's heart depends on his being blessed with the right nightmares. The result, according to Diamond, is that he gains an understanding of himself as being "bound towards death." And this entails a sense for others as his "fellow passengers to the grave," rather than as alien creatures "bound on separate journeys." To be human, then, one must imaginatively own one's own humanity, and this seems closely interconnected with the capacity for enjoying life, for love or mirth, which so many of Dickens's characters have suppressed or rejected.

> The first thing that Dickens's Scrooge does when he is fully awake is *laugh.* The laughter Dickens wants from his

> readers is the laughter of awakened humanity in us. . . . Dickens's aims are not unlike those explicitly put by Joseph Conrad: If a writer of fiction takes a particular moment of life and holds it up and "shows it in its vibration, its colour, its form," shows "the stress and passion" of it, this may awaken in the heart of the reader, the beholder of the described moment, "that feeling of unavoidable solidarity; of the solidarity in mysterious origin, in toil, in hope, in uncertain fate, which binds men to each other and all mankind to the visible world."[26]

In addition to a felt sense of interconnectedness or solidarity, a broader and more penetrating sensibility also entails a perception of the *malum,* of the tearing of life's precious fabric. The philosopher Hans Jonas tells us that this is basic to the emergence of responsibility and the idea of the good. Jonas writes,

> as long as [a] danger is unknown, we do not know what to preserve and why. Knowledge . . . comes . . . from the perception of what to avoid. This is perceived first and teaches us, by the revulsion of feeling which acts ahead of knowledge, to apprehend the value whose antithesis so affects us. We know the thing is at stake only when we know that it is at stake. Because this is the way we are made: the perception of the malum is infinitely easier to us than the perception of the bonum.[27]

A humane and realistic sensibility is one that is not too busy or too occupied with goals, plans, and objectives to apprehend and to feel the grossly destructive violations: the mother holding her starving child, the terrorist bomb that explodes on a busy sidewalk, the most recent attempt at "ethnic cleansing," the dead fish floating along the banks of a putrid harbor.

A better mysticism, a more penetrating attentiveness, supports a felt sense of interconnectedness, a perception of the *malum,* and an inkling of the good. Here, for example, we may note that, while General Dwight D. Eisenhower was the accomplished military manager who coordinated the great and crucially successful invasion of Europe, he was also a man of sensibility who, during the spring of 1944 and thereafter, occasionally was visited by his own spirits. The following lines from one of his biographies communicate this, and they also contrast rather sharply with the sports-talk and leadership-speak about winning in business and in life, Jesus as chief executive, and how to live your life according to a strategic plan.

> Eisenhower had such a keen sense of family, of the way in which each casualty meant a grieving family back home. . . . In 1964, when he was filming with Walter Cronkite a television special entitled "D-Day Plus 20," Cronkite asked him what he thought about when he returned to Normandy. In reply, he spoke not about the tanks, the guns, the planes, the ships, the personalities of his commanders and their opponents, or the victory. Instead he spoke of the families of the men buried in the American cemetery in Normandy. He said that he could never come to this spot without thinking of how blessed he and Mamie were to have grandchildren, and how much it saddened him to think of all the couples in America who had never had that blessing, because their only son was buried in France.[28]

A better mysticism entails a kind of sacramental resonance with the intricate and delicate web of life, a touching on the mysteries of care and pain, of beauty, and of belonging to a wider universe. It means a sensibility that engages the everyday and the practical partly because it knows that all of the sinews and the surfaces connect with something more. It means a felt sense of interdependent interrelatedness, of the *malum* and the good. It means the arresting of our attention by the familiar and astounding pulse of stars, planets, ecologies, landscapes, neighborhoods, promises, threats, hopes, fears, terrors, and joys.

The American philosopher Charles Saunders Peirce once commended "musement,"—an activity, he said, that "involves no purpose save that of casting aside all serious purpose." Musement, which Peirce distinguished sharply from *a*musement, means letting things, people, ideas, and events strike us without immediately imposing on them an order born of specific tasks and objectives. Having commended musement, however, Peirce then calculated exactly how much time we should spend at it (five to six percent of our waking hours, or forty to forty-five minutes per day).[29] Calculated musement—this seems a curious testimony to the persistent hold of management on the American psyche. And yet on musement of a less fettered sort (or else something rather like it) hangs the possibility of extending contemporary attentiveness and sensibility beyond narrowed managerial bounds.

A BETTER MYTHOLOGY

In addition to being informed by a better mysticism, interesting conversations about leadership also will be informed by a better mythology, a richer picture of human beings in the world, their possibilities, and their limits. These conversations will draw on a broader, less single-minded, more complicated and dynamic view of people and their circumstances, abilities, motives, and prospects than generally is supported by the social Darwinist–*laissez faire* myth of ceaseless competition. My own judgment is that this better mythology will contain at least three related elements that build on the broader, more penetrating sensibility that we have just outlined.

One element is the fact that people wield significant but nonetheless limited powers. Humans occupy a distinctive place in the world. We depend on physical and biological processes that brought our species into being and that continue to sustain us. As individuals and communities, we depend on historical and social processes and contexts. We find ourselves involved in interdependent interrelations with other people, with institutions, and with environments. We are acted upon and influenced by other actors and conditions, and we also act upon and influence other actors and conditions. Our specific possibilities for action depend on a combination of elements that are present on particular occasions and in particular contexts.[30]

This is not to say that we are simply fated. Human decisions and actions make a difference in how things turn out. Almost no one can surf the Internet, walk into a modern medical center, or ride in a jet plane and gaze out the window at the checkerboard pattern of cultivated lands in the American midwest without recognizing that, both as individuals and as groups, we are equipped with impressive powers and capacities. On the other hand, we clearly do not control all outcomes and events. There are things we cannot change and, as any Internet surfer, medical patient, airline passenger, or farmer knows, there are always unintended consequences. The reason for this is that we do not act alone or in a vacuum. There are always other actors and additional conditions.

This is a bit of wisdom shared by people in vastly different circumstances. Some years ago outside a shelter called Freedom House in Richmond, Virginia, I spoke with a woman who had gathered up her young son and fled an abusive partner. She was chain-smoking and nervous. She realized that she had acted, and that her act could make a difference for herself and her child. She also knew that she was taking a risk, and that things might turn out differently than she intended. She was not sure what her estranged partner might do. She did not know where she and her child could stay. She did not know whether temporary assistance was available from local agencies and institutions. As she put it, after more than a year of brooding without preparing and without a plan, "I just went for it, you know?"

To return to an earlier illustration, General Eisenhower didn't get much rest on the night of June 5, 1944. After more than a year of planning, organizing, politicking, setting goals, and discussing objectives, he was deciding to launch the largest amphibious assault in history. He had the advantage of clear superiority in the air, but as he pondered the tides, the weather, and the potential actions of his captains and battalions, of Charles de Gaulle, and of the German defenders, he knew that he could neither control nor anticipate all relevant outcomes. Like the woman with whom I spoke in Richmond, he was taking a risk.[31]

The second element is the fact that persons, communities, and institutions are caught up in fragmentation and conflict. The varieties of human misorientation and destructiveness are protean. True, we wield very significant powers and abilities. Evidences of human creativity, achievement, and heartfelt sensitivity abound. Nonetheless, even our best achievements, both as individuals and as communities, remain inextricably intertwined with disturbing commitments, broken trusts, and chronic transgressions. And, very often, we clearly are not at our best.

So, for example, even caring parents sometimes neglect and inappropriately manipulate their children, and there are many parents who participate deficiently in, or even flagrantly violate, important familial obligations. Even a relatively just and prosperous society will tend to regard other cultures almost exclusively through the spectacles of its own partial interests; occasionally, it will simply demonize whoever and whatever is foreign. And, then again, many societies are neither relatively just nor prosperous. Our global economy can be enormously productive, and it often furnishes people with needed goods, increased freedoms, and enhanced opportunities. But it has also littered the earth with notorious imbalances, injustices, sufferings, and ecological disasters. The deep, sometimes chilling ambiguity of our advancements in science, technology, and production is one of the more profound lessons of modern history.

Here we come across an element of wisdom that supports a pessimistic realism. When once we apprehend that ours is a world of chronic fragmentation and conflict where life and its integrity constantly are threatened, we also begin to understand the need for courts of law that deter abusive partners as well as for amphibious assaults that subvert totalitarian designs. We see the need for regular checks and restraints. We know why so many are buried at Normandy, even though it saddens us to remember them and their families. We appreciate the importance of relationships and institutions structured around clear statements of responsibilities. We will not be too quick to dismantle balances of power that sometimes inhibit egregious harm.

The third element is the great nevertheless. In a world of fragmentation, misorientation, conflict, and destruction, nevertheless possibilities for good abound. Perhaps you are acquainted with the routinely moving fidelity of a husband who cares for his wife through years of trying illness. Perhaps we have knowledge of a community that housed and hid hunted strangers in the midst of Nazi terror, and at significant risk to itself (as did the village of Le Chambon-sur-Lignon in occupied France).[32] Perhaps one encounters a corporation that strives to attend to the interests of shareholders, but also the interests of long-term employees, customers, and various other publics affected by its operations. Perhaps we find that, once we reduce the onslaught of pollution, profligate development, and misuse, at least some severely damaged ecosystems significantly improve (a fragile process that appears to be underway in some waterways in the eastern United States). Or perhaps we are acquainted with an organization and a movement that pursued a course of nonviolent resistance and confrontation in order to advance the participation of an oppressed minority and also witness to the possibility of a more just society. (Recall the efforts of Martin Luther King Jr. on behalf of both civil rights for African Americans and the betterment of poor people in America.)[33]

Acquaintances and encounters such as these also contain important seeds of wisdom. Like the story of Scrooge's nighttime conversion, they point toward a more capacious generosity and responsibility. They point toward possibilities for more abundant life. They therefore encourage us in efforts to make things better, to risk strategies for motivating and guiding persons and groups in paths of more genuine attentiveness and fidelity. They encourage an optimistic temper. Precisely in the midst of a world of lost possibilities, debilitating threats, and massive suffering, they indicate that there are reasons to hope.

BEYOND LEADERSHIP-SPEAK

Slam-dunking your way to success. ManagePro 3.1. Winning at the game of life. Inner peace through strategic planning. Even Jesus turns out to be a chief executive.

You and I live in a time and place where a shallow and reductive leadership-speak has insinuated itself into business, sports, politics, education, spirituality, and more. But this does not mean that we are simply fated to repeat the corrosive rhetoric of the age. There are resources on which we may draw in order to ponder alternatives. Even as we acknowledge the importance of appropriate planning, strategizing, management, and assessment, not all of our conversations about leadership must be confined within the narrow bounds of management models and *laissez faire.*

Informed by a better mysticism and a more proper attentiveness, by enlightening nightmares, right revulsions, and purposeless musings, we may sense that the point of life is more a matter of communion than of manipulation, and that our actions, plans, and strategies appropriately are ordered to that more fundamental and compelling point. We may envision a world in which relationships and interconnections are themselves part of the meaningful point of life rather than merely means to strategic objectives. If I may be allowed a directly religious allusion, we may suggest that truly humane leadership will picture the chief end of life more along the lines of a nourishing and common meal (say, a Seder or Lord's Supper) than of a meticulously planned, executed, and evaluated management system.

Moreover, informed by a better mythology, we may reject the notion that life *is* competition in favor of the more complicated view that life is limited freedom situated in the midst of interactive interdependencies, plagued by tendencies toward fragmentation and conflict, and yet blessed with possibilities for truer sensibility and community. We may therefore insist that, even as genuine leaders appreciate the importance of action and effort, they also remember that all things are not always possible, that persons and communities sometimes are caught in straits and circumstances beyond their own doing and undoing. We may note that genuine leadership often draws on an appropriate pessimism, a realistic sense that is not surprised by defeats and tragedies and terrors. We may insist that good leaders be realists who anticipate the need to restrain evil and also to limit the powers of persons, groups, and institutions by dispersing and balancing powers. And, *nevertheless,* we may also suggest that leadership is hopeful. We may also say that a good leader is often an optimist who ventures a creative act, who risks in order to make things better. Like the woman I met at Freedom House in Richmond, like Dwight Eisenhower in 1944, a leader is someone who steps out in hope.

Part 1

A Theology of Hopeful Realism

2 Envisioning God and Ourselves

The nineteenth-century theologian Friedrich Schleiermacher once wrote that where there is disagreement and controversy, it can never be superfluous to begin by saying what conception of theology is being employed.[1] His point is more pertinent now than he could have imagined. There is little agreement today about the proper subject matter and tasks of theology.[2] Some envision theology as the reflective work of particular churches, whereas others attempt global or world theologies that transcend even the great religious traditions. Many remain convinced that theologians reflect on divine revelation, whereas others insist that theology is our human effort to fashion imaginative constructs that furnish practical guidance. Some regard theology primarily as a matter of identifying patterns in biblical narratives. Others write theologies that seem decisively shaped by analyses of current circumstances and conversations with political philosophies. Still others link theology rather closely with new scientific theories and findings.

THEOLOGY

My purpose here is to present Christian theology as a reflective enterprise that helps us to envision God and ourselves. In my judgment, theology is a sort of practical reasoning. A theologian tries to help persons and communities interact with objects, situations, and realities in a manner that is faithfully responsive to God. This practical aim, in turn, requires an imaginative interpretation of the objects, situations, and realities with which we interact. It requires that we bring images, ideas, and patterns to bear on our experiences. In short, it requires an interpretive vision or strong reading of things in relation to God.[3]

Theology is a reflective enterprise whereby religious communities attempt to envision in relation to God the many situations and realities with which we interact. The forms of theology are particular rather than generic because specific religious communities and their heritages furnish distinct poetries or sense-making resources. Thus, Jewish communities and traditions furnish interpretive resources for Jewish theologies, Islamic communities and traditions furnish interpretive resources for Muslim theologies, and so on. A Christian theologian engages the historic resources of the Christian movement. She or he works with the many symbols, images, ideas, and patterns that emerge in the church's scriptures, traditions, and contemporary life in order to portray the world, our possibilities, and our limits in relation to God. She or he makes use of the church's poetry in order to envision the encompassing reality in which we live and move.[4]

By Christian theology, then, I mean a practical and interpretive discourse that aims at an appropriate degree of definiteness and coherence but remains closely interconnected with the languages of faith and piety.[5] I mean a sense-making intellectual enterprise concerning affections and emotions that put us in touch with compelling realities. I mean a faithful reflection that evokes wonder, encourages us to ask anew about the divine object in our experiences, tries to envision the world and our place in it, and so helps us to reorient life and practice. I mean a historically particular and convictional wisdom that is borne by Christian communities and their traditions, and that helps us to ponder God and ourselves.

When understood in this way, Christian theology is more sacramental than technical. It retains the sense—too often lost in the modern West—that we are near neighbors of the transcendent and that the circumference of our lives remains permeable to something more. It eschews vocabularies that claim to offer detached descriptions of things completely known, and instead it traffics in images, patterns, models, and paradigms that interpret but never entirely capture.[6] Theology therefore often has more in common with sermons, hymns, and prayers than it does with many academic monographs and treatises. It makes common cause with works of art and literature that "quicken into lit presence the continuum between temporality and eternity,"[7] between human beings and the other.

Theology becomes more highly disciplined and reflective, not when we misguidedly try to translate symbols into literal terms, but when we articulate a framework, network, or system of interlocking symbols, a doctrinal schema that yields a coherent outlook. Then, the reflective poetry of Christian theology expresses a distinct apprehension of God. Then, it presents a distinctive vision or strong reading of our many relationships, institutions, loyalties, loves, sufferings, and involvements. Then, it offers an interpretation or construal of life that can and should be brought into conversation with other interpretations and construals that are current and influential.[8]

It is important to remember that the doctrinal network of Christian theology is shaped and sustained by communities that bear particular heritages. Images and patterns are drawn from scriptures, creeds, confessions, liturgies, the writings of earlier theologians, and so on. Thus, symbolic resources that others in the past have both developed and found illuminating continue to inform the Christian community, its orientation, and its vision in the present. This is why there is always a conservative aspect to Christian theology. Good theology requires respect for those who have gone before, as well as sustained attention to received paradigms, symbols, and interpretations.[9]

Nevertheless, the fundamental concern is not antiquarian. Christian theology furnishes symbolic resources in order to address the life of faith today. Like a preacher, it tries to interpret the current lives and circumstances of particular persons and communities in the light of a religious message. Theology aims at a clarification of life.[10] It tries to illumine experiences, relationships, and structures in our present context. It tries to help us think cogently in our present context and to negotiate life in our present context. This is why, even as it attends to past traditions, Christian theology always also probes complexities, dynamics, and threats in our current culture and circumstance. It suggests that here and now there is something more and something other going on than often meets the eye.

Christian theology is able to suggest this because, in all of its interpretations of past traditions and current circumstances, the peculiar objects of its inquiry are God and ourselves.[11] This is the something more and something other to which theology points. This is what it tries to help us think cogently about, and this is what it tries to help us discern in our present situation.

It is in this sense that Christian theology aims at "a reality more real than appearances."[12] Theology tries to pierce the surface and to suggest an extraordinary vision. It points to the circumambiency in which we live and move. By intensifying, redescribing, and reenvisioning our interactions in the world, Christian theology tries to help us see things in a different way. It testifies to the depth of things, and it insists that the concrete realities of our experiences point beyond themselves toward the other. It witnesses to a real presence and power in, with, and under the ordinary and pragmatic.[13] It brings us to a threshold and it exposes us to a divine ordering.

POETIC LICENSE

I should also mention that, in this respect, Christian theology is not much at home in our time. Next to a modern technical sensibility that reduces all experiences and realities to a single, calculable, and utilitarian surface (the "Formica-ization" of existence), it necessarily seems out of place—the quaint and perhaps also haunting survival of classical passion and piety in a cold and empty world of entirely instrumental, means-and-ends reasoning. But it is equally ill at ease where the iron cage of technical empiricism has been exchanged for more current linguistic boxes in which words refer only to other words, and where the sentence and the image have meaning only by virtue of their internal relations within the language game or system. Against this new reduction and the consequent loss of faith in any reality beyond our words, the reflective poetry of Christian theology still claims to refer, to point, to respond to the radical actuality of things. It continues to maintain that word and world belong together and indeed that, in some sense, word connects world and God.[14]

From this vantage point, the iron cage of technical empiricism as well as the more current linguistic boxes entail some mistaken, theologically disastrous assumptions. They assume that we alone act to purpose, and therefore that we alone bestow meaning and value. In effect, they presume that we create our own worlds.

How so? On the one hand, we may presume to create our own world technically, by fashioning an artificial, secondary environment. We may manipulate raw materials according to our own purposes and designs, and then mistake the world for our own product. This confusion results from the assumption that what we purposefully manipulate is ethically neutral and axiologically inert. Our secondary environment therefore comprises the entire realm of meaning, purpose, and value. It becomes the only realm within which and to which we meaningfully respond, and we no longer ask whether and how it meaningfully and appropriately responds to anything other than itself. Similarly, we may also create our own world linguistically. We may interpret and construe things by means of our particular language system, and then mistake the world for our own linguistic construct. The confusion here results from the assumption that meaning, purpose, and value are functions of language alone. Our language system alone therefore determines the realm in which and to which we meaningfully respond, and we no longer ask whether and how our language system meaningfully and appropriately responds to anything other than itself.

Either way, the practically relevant world, the world of meaning and value in which we live and move, becomes almost entirely one of our own making. Human power and intelligence, whether technical or linguistic, determine what is as well as what ought to be. We might say that the world beyond our technical and linguistic manipulations doesn't come up on our screens because it remains without meaningful trajectories, purposes, or signs with which we might appropriately or inappropriately interact. It has no meaningful presence, and so it can neither mediate nor point toward encounters with an Other.

Much more might be said about this. For one thing, in a theological perspective, both technical empiricism and reductive linguistic turns celebrate human power, intelligence, and technique as the sole arbiters of meaning and value. They deny that we are creatures and instead suggest ways in which we may try to become like gods. They therefore lend renewed and haunting relevance to the story of the Tower of Babel.[15] Here, however, I want to emphasize a relationship between certain philosophical assumptions and some theological claims.

The philosophical assumptions that the world is neither merely our technical product nor our linguistic construct point toward a world that "pushes back." They indicate a world of meaningful presence where we find ourselves interacting with other things and persons whose meaning and value we neither simply construct nor control. They also encourage us to identify patterns in our interactions. In short, this amounts to a philosophical realism that presumes that we are in touch with a world beyond ourselves, that we are able to know this world and reflect on it, and that our judgments about values are intertwined with our knowledge of objects, processes, and occurrences. But it is not yet a theology. Theology takes an additional step. It claims that, in and through our patterned interactions with the many others that push back, we find ourselves interacting with an Other.[16]

This is why Christian theology claims to be more than a linguistic framework centered on the character "God" as rendered in scriptural narratives. This is also why it claims to be more than an imaginative construct that lends orientation to human life and in which the name "God" functions as the ultimate point of reference.[17] To be sure, Christian theology attends to images and patterns cast up by scripture and orients human life in the world. It envisions, but in its envisioning it also takes poetic license. It refuses technical hubris and linguistic agnosticism. It claims to pierce the technical and linguistic surfaces. It claims to construe a world of realities that push back, and it claims that in and through these others we find ourselves interacting with an Other. Christian theology claims to refer, to express, and to point. And the object of theological wisdom, the reality, radical actuality, and circumambiency to which it points, is our existence in, with, and before God, the living relation or encounter between God and ourselves that comprises the depth of our present circumstance and of every circumstance.

CREATION, SIN, PROVIDENCE, AND REDEMPTION

Consider the doctrine of original sin.[18] Here is a traditional symbol, connected with Paul's letter to the Romans as well as with early chapters of Genesis, that was developed by classical theologians such as Augustine and John Calvin. Understood poetically, it does not require claims about the historicity of Adam and Eve or, for that matter, about the historicity of any figure in Genesis 2:4 through 11:9. Neither does it entail implausible theories of how sin's contagion is transmitted from one generation to the next. Properly understood, original sin is an interpretive image or symbol. It helps us to envision the actuality of life-before-God-and-God-before-life.

As such, original sin indicates that, in and through experiences both ordinary and horrifying, we apprehend a human fault, and that the fault is both radical and universal. There is no sin-free human capacity and there is no sin-free person, community, or institution. Original sin construes our passionate pessimism, sorrow, and grief at human history as an epic of violence, fragmentation, and conflict. (This, we might say, is one of the major points of Genesis 2:4 through 11:9. The children of the first human pair are the first murderer and the first murder victim. This is not the most cheerful beginning. And, then, violent gangs roam the earth, which is why Lamech avenges seventy-sevenfold. Despite a clean slate and a new beginning after the flood, "the whole earth" migrates from the east and attempts to "make a name for ourselves" by building a tower to the heavens.)[19] The symbol of original sin helps us to envision the entire human project as chronically and unavoidably skewed, and it points to our apprehensions of God as judge in and through the many destructive consequences of our sinful misorientation and constriction.[20]

The extended bit of epic poetry we call the doctrine of original sin means that, to some extent and degree, the story of multifaceted corruption and judgment is the story of "everyperson" and of every human community. We find that we unavoidably are devoted to the wrong things or else to the right things wrongly. We find that we so concentrate on our isolated causes and commitments that we inevitably fail to attend to the wider community of things in their mutual interdependence and common dependence on God. We find that we chronically transgress and fail to participate faithfully in the relationships of interdependence and trust in which we stand. In short, as both individuals and groups, we diminish life in its fullness, and we travel along the way toward death.

But this is not all there is to be said. Within the symbolic framework of Christian theology, the doctrine of sin never stands alone. It functions as a part of a wider fabric, and so it must always be understood in connection with the great symbols of creation, providence, and redemption.[21]

When we come upon the creation of the world and humankind in the Bible, we find both interconnection and distinction. Put bluntly, the connectedness is that humans are animals who, as do all other animals, depend on a slew of interdependent processes and conditions. As all other creatures do, they reproduce in their kind. They are blessed with the promise of progeny and a future that is common to animal and plant life. Humans, like all other creatures, are parts of the articulated and good whole that is God's creation.

The distinction is that humans exercise powers that other species on earth do not. They are fitted with significant capacities for interventions into the world. They participate in the wider, interconnected, and ordered whole of creation in ways that other creatures do not. (This should be apparent to anyone who has read Psalm 8 and also looked down on the checkerboard pattern of Indiana farmland from a jet at thirty thousand feet.) And yet (as virtually every farmer and airline passenger also knows), these remain the capacities of creatures who are enmeshed in the web of created interrelations, who continue to depend on it, and who are unable to anticipate and control all relevant outcomes.[22]

Considered symbolically, creation does not refer to a particular theory about the origin of the world so much as it interprets and envisions our experience of life and the world as gifts as well as our experience as limited and dependent creatures within a larger ordered cosmos. "God saw everything that he had made, and indeed, it was very good" (Gen. 1:31). The doctrine of creation indicates that humans are created good and are intended to occupy a distinctive and creative place in the dynamic whole of God's good world. We are equipped with significant, even wondrous, powers and capacities. We are fitted for conscious, intentional, creative, and faithful interrelations with God and with others. We are created for an abundant and good life of true communion with God in community with others.

The doctrine of God's good creation points to our apprehensions of God in and through our experiences of given structures, capacities, possibilities, and limits. Among other things, then, it reminds us that God is not only a judge, and that sin (although powerful and pervasive) is *not* the way it's supposed to be. Under the sway of sin, the life for which we are fitted is truncated and constricted. As John Calvin put it, "sin is not our nature but its derangement."[23]

Providence helps us to envision God as continuing to uphold, govern, and preserve even a world gone awry. Thus, in Psalm 104:24–30, Calvin noted that "living things both small and great . . . all look to [God] to give them food in due season."[24] We continue to be upheld by dependable constancies and regular operations in the natural world, as well as by reliable persons, communities, and institutions. Moreover, God does not simply abandon creatures to the consequences of misorientation. Despite sin's corruption, for example, we retain significant intellectual and technical abilities, as well as moral sensibilities and capacities that enhance life and also enable important levels of human flourishing. In addition, we find that our destructive tendencies and designs are sometimes checked; occasionally, if also unintentionally, they even issue in good consequences.[25]

Finally, the great symbol of redemption helps us to envision the transformation of life and its deliverance from diminution and destruction. If sin means death, then redemption means new creation and newness of life (2 Cor. 5:17; Rom. 6). If sin means a shrinking away, then redeeming grace means an enlargement and re-turning of persons toward true communion and community. If sin means an impelling tendency toward corruption, then redeeming grace means the emergence of a new tendency. Indeed, we may say that, as redeemer, Jesus Christ teaches, embodies, and empowers *life*. He is the prophet who teaches love of God and neighbor. He is the pioneer and perfecter who remains loyal to God and others. By his reconciling work in the midst of fragmentation and conflict, he empowers the good and abundant life of true communion with God in community with others for which we are fitted and that characterizes the reign of God.

Especially within the framework of our encounter with God in Jesus Christ, the person-for-others, we therefore find that events and realities—both terrible and inspiring—sometimes become occasions of redeeming grace. We envision traces of God's reconciling activity in the world. For example, the suffering of innocent children, particularly in connection with our own childhood memories of parents who cared for us as well as our own experiences as parents, may help to push our corrupted visions beyond a parochial focus on our own isolated interests. Costly consequences of devotions to wrong causes as well as compelling instances of costly faithfulness to appropriate ones may bend the arcs of our hearts beyond persistent constrictions. Disturbing lies and injustices as well as trusts, obligations, and principles splendidly kept sometimes encourage creative reconfigurings of human responsibility. In short, even as we are caught in the grip of sin's warping tendency, we apprehend the reconciling activity of God that is decisively disclosed in Jesus Christ and that continues to present possibilities for reorientation and renewal. Despite our radical and universal fault, despite the validity of our pessimism, sorrow, and grief, grace abounds, and there is reason to hope.[26]

HOPEFUL REALISM

The general outlook or vision supported by this medley of symbols may be described as a hopeful realism. This is an outlook that acknowledges our significant but limited and dependent powers and capabilities; that expects diminishment, conflict, fragmentation, and death; but that does not fail to look for enlargement, reconciliation, and life. Hopeful realism recognizes the persistently destructive bents as well as the promising possibilities of all persons, communities, and institutions. It therefore subjects all of them to criticism even as it affirms them all. It summons all to repentance as well as to an ethic of faithful participation that respects and enhances the good and abundant life of true communion with God in community with others.

Now it is precisely this general outlook, vision, and orientation, rather than any isolated or single symbol, that finally envisions, interprets, and points to life in, with, and before God. Creation suggests that, as we exercise our powers and capacities, we encounter God as the creator, source, and fountain of existence who orders the interdependent conditions, possibilities, and limits on which we depend. And, indeed, this encounter also intimates the appropriateness of true communion in community. Yet creation alone misses not only the tragic diminution and perversion of life and its given possibilities but also the dramatic interaction in human history between destructive misdirection and creative transformation. The doctrine of sin points to our chronic corruptions as well as to our encounters with God as judge in and through their destructive consequences. Taken alone, however, the doctrine of sin ends in a shallow pessimism that fails to apprehend and express the tragedy of life, its continuing possibilities, and—beyond tragedy—its passionate hope. Again, providence directs us toward apprehensions of God in and through the abilities, sensibilities, structures, and occurrences that continue to sustain us. Redemption directs us toward interactions with God as redeemer, the gracious bringer of transformation and new life. But apart from creation and sin, these symbols lose their preserving and restorative dimensions; they become detached from a sense of lost possibilities and debilitating threats. They no longer evoke hope where hope is most severely tested—namely, in a world of fragmentation, conflict, and death.

Within a Christian doctrinal framework, then, our thinking about God and ourselves becomes distorted whenever one or another of these symbols is torn away from the wider poetic fabric. The meaning of each depends on its interconnections with all. This is why the reflective poetry of Christian theology attempts to hold these and other symbols together in an appropriate balance: the many symbols need to be organized into a single framework if they are to express and enrich an adequate sense for the divine reality with whom we deal in all of our many dealings.

Where this is accomplished, where these symbols genuinely are held together in an appropriate balance, there emerges a religious vision that situates human life and the world in the midst of something more. Then the hopefully realistic poetry of Christian theology does indeed portray an encompassing reality more real than appearances. It construes, expresses, and interprets this radical actuality as God (the creator, judge, sustainer, and redeemer) and ourselves (the good, dependent, somewhat capable but also radically corrupted creatures who nevertheless are sustained and even redeemed). It points toward a divine ordering in, with, and under all that is ordinary and pragmatic, and it authorizes an ethic of faithful participation in response to the divine ordering.

Moreover, precisely because it orients human beings in the present and precisely because it makes claims about the living relation and encounter that comprise the depth of every circumstance, Christian theology also needs to be developed in connection with current situations and realities. Precisely because it claims to support a participatory ethic that responds to the radical actuality of things, it needs to engage culture, society, and world. Theology calls for a continuing interaction between symbol and experience that promises to enrich both faithfulness and vision.

How, in the midst of our present environment, does God come to us in worship, work, and prayer? How do we experience the corruptions of sin and the promises of grace in a postmodern age of burgeoning technology, increasing global interdependence, and renewed attention to particular communities and traditions? How do we encounter God as judge and as redeemer in the midst of massive starvation, struggles for liberation, and traditional hatreds that threaten fragile prospects even for tolerably just and survivable societies?

Again, we also need to ask how the outlook articulated by Christian theology interacts with other outlooks. How does it differ from naive optimisms and overconfident humanisms that routinely end in cynicism and despair? How does it compare with unrelieved pessimisms that issue in stoical counsels of detachment? How does it regard *laissez faire* ideologies of ceaseless competition? How does it interact with the agnostic indifference to the theological and metaphysical that often accompany the modern sense that, whether technologically or linguistically, we simply create our own worlds? To what extent may a hopeful Christian realism make common cause with and also be instructed by contemporary ecological sensibilities and feminist movements? Does it endorse struggles for the international and intercultural recognition of human rights? Only by confronting questions such as these can the reflective poetry of Christian theology furnish resources for thinking cogently about God and ourselves in our contemporary environment.

CONSERVATIVE AND PROGRESSIVE, WORLDLY AND POETIC

We live in interesting times. Conservatives challenge us to maintain the integrity of our confessions, and they lament the theological amnesia that is bound to beset Christian communities that neglect their traditions. Progressives challenge us to engage current circumstances: questions about sexuality and gender, religious pluralism, environmental threats, shifting configurations of international powers, new economic interdependencies, and more. They worry that worn-out practices and ideas will subvert the dynamism of our faithful witness. Those who understand Christian theology as a reflection on the church's poetry have good reasons to take both of these challenges very seriously.[27] Indeed, they will encourage Christians and their communities to advance a *living* tradition, to discern a fresh dynamism and complexity of meaning in classic Christian symbols without adopting defensive postures that dismiss needed reinterpretations.

Again, as I understand it, Christian theology will aid and advance an engaging and participatory faithfulness. It will favor a kind of "worldly Christianity" that does not shy away from compelling challenges, complexities, and ambiguities. It will engage cultures both critically and constructively. It will encourage a hopeful Christian realism that refuses to retreat into a new otherworldliness precisely because it believes that this is *God's* world, and that, despite sin's diminution and fragmentation of the abundant and good life that befits us, the steadfast God is not absent from any part of the human project.

Finally, a note about manner of presentation. Theological texts should keep in touch with the church's poetry and its originating symbols. They should contribute to the sense that we inhabit a world of encompassing presence as well as many dimensions, thresholds, vitalities, and meanings. They should intimate something more in, with, and under the familiar and astounding sacrament of stars, planets, ecologies, landscapes, neighborhoods, promises, threats, hopes, fears, terrors, and glories. However partially and inadequately, they should point to an Other who meets us at every turn.

3 The Sense the Trinity Makes

"Glory be to the Father, and to the Son, and to the Holy Spirit." Such trinitarian language has never been free of controversy. For many Jews and Muslims, the Trinity smacks of tritheism or the affirmation of three gods. Among Christians, unitarian movements that deny the Trinity frequently have arisen. There are nontrinitarian denominations in America today, and probably more nontrinitarians in the pews of officially trinitarian churches than we often realize. Moreover, from early centuries to the present, theologians who affirm the Trinity have often disagreed about basic terms and concepts.[1] Small wonder that more than a few people regard trinitarian doctrine as the quintessential statement of Christian nonsense: 1 + 1 + 1 = 1.

Does the Trinity make any sense? Yes, but not as a kind of celestial mathematics or "an esoteric exposition of God's inner life."[2] The Trinity is a bit of faithful reflection that points to God and ourselves.[3] As such, it emerges from a biblically initiated exploration into God and redemption, and it expresses a saving knowledge that lends us the confidence to participate faithfully in God's world. It expresses, interprets, and summarizes the Christian community's distinctive, threefold apprehension of life-before-God-and-God-before-life, and it points to the God who remains beyond our comprehension.

A BIBLICALLY INITIATED EXPLORATION

"I believe in God the Father Almighty, Maker of heaven and earth, and in Jesus Christ his only Son our Lord. . . . I believe in the Holy Spirit." The Trinity was given classical expression in early local church creeds, such as the one developed by the church at Rome that forms the basis for our Apostles' Creed, and in the creed adopted at Nicea in 325 C.E. that was later expanded at Constantinople in 381 C.E.[4] But the creeds did not invent trinitarian reflection. Responding to important challenges in the Greco-Roman world, they continued an exploration that began with biblical communities.

The Hebrew Scriptures intimate notable complexities in God's relationship with the world and with persons and communities. Here we find the affirmation that God is one (Deut. 6:4). We also find references to the spirit of God as a powerful agent of creation and life (Gen. 1:2; Ps. 33:6; Ezek. 37:1–10), as an empowering source of inspiration for leaders, judges, kings, and prophets, and as God's presence enabling the covenant community to live according to the commandments (Ezek. 36:27).[5] Recently, several scholars also have pointed to the importance of the figure of Woman Wisdom who originates from God, has a role in the act of creation, instructs humanity, and offers peace and security (Prov. 1–9).[6] Nevertheless, Hebrew monotheism may be characterized as comparatively unitarian. The trinitarian symbol itself emerges from an exploration into God and redemption among New Testament communities.

Early Christians faced a fundamental theological problem. From Judaism, they accepted the conviction that God is the one creator, governor, and deliverer who alone is worthy of worship and praise. Indeed, Jesus himself points to "our Father in heaven" whose name is to be hallowed, who feeds birds and clothes lilies, who creates all things and also faithfully sustains them, and whose historic reign shall culminate in the coming kingdom (Matt. 6:9–13, 6:25–34; Mark 1:15). Yet early Christians also believed that in Christ, the crucified and resurrected one, "there is a new creation; everything old has passed away; see everything has become new" (2 Cor. 5:17). How were they to make sense of this decisive experience of reconciliation, redemption, and renewal in the context of their monotheistic conviction?

Out of their wrestling with this question, Christians came to understand Jesus of Nazareth to be paradigmatic and decisive for experiences of God, grace, and redemption. Jesus is the Messiah or the Christ, the one who proclaims the advent of God's reign and the one in whom that saving reality is made manifest. He is the exalted "Son of Man" who will return with the clouds of heaven (Mark 13:26); the second Adam who succeeds where the first failed (Rom. 5:12–19; 1 Cor. 15:45); the teacher who delivers perfect wisdom (Matt. 5–7); the pioneer and perfecter of our faith (Heb. 12:2). His cross is the power of God (1 Cor. 1:18). Jesus Christ is Lord and Savior.

Images multiply. In Colossians, the "Lord Jesus Christ" is "the image of the invisible God, the firstborn of all creation" in whom all things hold together (Col. 1:3, 15–17). In Revelation, he is the slain Lamb who is both Alpha and Omega (Rev. 22:13). Romans begins by speaking of "the gospel concerning [God's] Son, who was descended from David according to the flesh and was declared to be Son of God with power according to the Spirit of holiness by resurrection from the dead" (Rom. 1:3–4). In the Gospel of John, Jesus is the "only" son. He is the Logos, the Word of God who was in the beginning with God and through whom all things were made. He is the Word incarnate, the true life that was the light of all people, the light that shines in the darkness and has not been overcome (John 1:11–14).

In the light of Jesus' life, ministry, death, and resurrection, early Christians understood their experiences of redemption to have another dimension as well. They believed that the Spirit endowed Jesus with power as Messiah (Matt. 3:13–17; Mark 1:9–11; Luke 3:21–22; Matt. 12:28; Luke 4:16–21) and that, after his ascension, the Christian community was gathered and energized by the Spirit (Acts 2:1–21). Believers were baptized into the body of Christ, united with one another, and born into God's kingdom by the power of the Spirit (1 Cor. 12:13; John 3:1–9). Through the Spirit, both God and Christ continued to be present in the church (John 14). By the Spirit Christians received gifts of wisdom, knowledge, faith, healing, prophecy, discernment, tongues, and the interpretation of tongues (1 Cor. 12:4–11). In the Spirit they were sanctified and justified (1 Cor. 6:11); they experienced a new life of love, joy, and peace (Gal. 4:6, 5:22).

The early exploration into experiences of redemption and renewal therefore points to a threefold pattern, economy, or dynamic in the Christian community's experience of God in relation to us. The Father who reigns over all things meets us at every turn in both nature and history. Jesus the Christ is God's son and decisive act of re-creation and redemption, a light radiating into the world. The Spirit energizes, inspires, and empowers the new life of community, faith, and love. This pattern, economy, or dynamic is the impetus for trinitarian thinking, as well as the touchstone to which the best trinitarian theology always returns. It is also the basis for the missionary command at the end of Matthew's Gospel: "Go therefore and make disciples of all nations, baptizing them in the name of the Father and of the Son and of the Holy Spirit" (Matt. 28:19).

SAVING FAITH AND FAITHFUL PARTICIPATION

As the Christian movement spread around the Mediterranean basin, it encountered sharply dualistic beliefs. These beliefs were chiefly concerned with the cosmic redemption of the human spirit. They portrayed humans as immaterial souls bound to physical bodies that mired them in a world of change and suffering. Salvation meant release from both the physical body and the material world.

During the second century, Marcion of Pontus joined ideas such as these to Christian traditions. Marcion taught that the world was made of "beggarly elements." He was repulsed by sex and childbirth. He accepted the redeemer God that he discerned in New Testament writings, but rejected the Old Testament law and the creator God of Judaism. He claimed that the redeemer was unknown until Jesus Christ. He removed all acknowledgment of Old Testament authority from Paul's letters, as well as any identification of the creator as the Father of the Savior Jesus Christ, and he offered an expurgated Gospel of Luke as the only authentic Gospel.[7]

In this context, theological debates concerning Father, Son, and Spirit presented conflicting answers to the following questions: What sort of divine ordering meets us in the world? What kind of life is the new life of Christian faithfulness? Does it shun or disregard temporal, created existence? Few debates have had as many consequences for the Christian movement. Every dimension of Christian living is colored by the orthodox decision to regard the divine ordering as inclusive of material, nature, history, the physical body, family, children, commerce, and government as parts of the good creation in which loyalty to God's redeeming purpose encourages us to participate faithfully.

"I believe in God the Father Almighty, Maker of heaven and earth, and in Jesus Christ his only Son our Lord." Trinitarian belief identifies creator and redeemer. This is why it stands against Marcion's dualistic poetry of redemption. This is why it rejects dualistic rejections of the Hebrew Scriptures as well as dualistic devaluations of life in the world. Trinitarian theology retains the context of the Hebrew Scriptures and, indeed, insists that Jesus Christ and redemption cannot be understood apart from this context. It asserts that the creator who bears all things and in whom all things come to be is also the redeemer whose fundamental purpose is not suffering and decay but new life and true life. It affirms that this world is the good creation of the one most excellent God.

We must take this important affirmation an important step further if we are to understand a salvific dimension of trinitarian believing. Affirming that the power of reality who bears all things, in whom all things come to be, and in whom all things hold together is the good and faithful redeemer whose fundamental purpose is new life and true life leads to the affirmation that God is faithful. God is not loveless, thoughtless power. God is good to and for what God has brought into being. Indeed, God's purpose is new or renewed being.

Existentially, this affirmation entails a vivifying assurance and self-understanding. H. Richard Niebuhr noted that it expresses confidence in and loyalty to the one in whom we live and move and have our being.[8] It represents what Paul Tillich called "the courage to be," or what I prefer to call a courage to participate faithfully in God's great commonwealth of being despite the anxiety, doubt, and meaninglessness that beset us.[9] Trinitarian believing articulates saving faith.

This faith is saving because it delivers us from a destructive defensiveness. The self as sinner is an estranged, narrowed, and diminished self whose way of negotiating life is alienated and anxious. Much classical theology has claimed that the corrupted self either pridefully relies on its own strength in a hostile world or else slothfully abdicates responsibility in a threatening world. In any case, it becomes something other and less than it ought to be. It turns in on itself. It shrinks away from participatory relations with God and others. Saving faith reverses sin's diminishing and defensive movement. It delivers us from the deep distrust that causes us to envision all things as issuing from animosity or as a part of the realm of destruction. It brings the liberty to reenvision all that happens as part of a total divine activity, which includes death within the domain of life.[10]

"We trust in God the Holy Spirit, everywhere the giver and renewer of life."[11] This is how the Spirit gives and renews. This is how it empowers, and also how saving faith transforms. Faith and the Spirit turn the defensive, anxious self toward a renewed and true life. They insinuate the knowledge that the self is not an isolated or separate thing, but a relation to God and others, and they lend us the confidence and courage to participate faithfully—to recognize, respect, and enhance the good and abundant life of true communion with God in community with neighbor. This is part of the sense that trinitarian theology makes. It insists that the great God of glory is the good God of grace; and in this insistence, despite the travail and sorrow of life, it represents the participatory confidence and courage of saving faith.

A THREEFOLD APPREHENSION

Trinitarian theology continues a biblically initiated exploration. It articulates a knowledge of God's faithfulness that is basic to saving faith and participatory confidence. But this is not all. It also summarizes the Christian community's distinctive threefold apprehension of God and ourselves.

It does this by returning to the threefold pattern intimated in the New Testament. When we call God "the Father Almighty," we point to the God whose reign bears all of nature and history. We point to the Father of Jesus Christ, the all-governing one who faithfully creates, sustains, and redeems. We indicate the Other to whom we respond in every area and dimension of life and whose encompassing reign points toward Jesus' reconciling way with the world. When we call Jesus Christ the Son, the Logos, or Word of God, we affirm that in his self-emptying pattern and form he embodies and communicates the redemptive reality of God and of human life in appropriately responsive relation with God and others. We acknowledge that the particular way of life characterized by love of God and neighbor is truly fitted to the contours of God's reign, and that the new life of faithfulness requires us to follow in the way of Jesus Christ, the person-for-others. Finally, when we believe in the Holy Spirit, we acknowledge the vivifier and sanctifier present to us in experiences of reorientation and enlargement. We recognize the giver of life and new life who enables us to take up a faithfully participatory life of true communion with God in community with others. We acknowledge that the new life of faithfulness is one of being empowered to live in God's world in a manner that accords with God's redemptive way in Jesus Christ.

These three aspects of faith's experience cannot be equated or collapsed. Each is integral to the dynamic pattern and tendency of life-before-God-and-God-before-life. This is why trinitarian theology stands against three kinds of unitarianism.[12]

It stands against a unitarianism of the Father, the maker of heaven and earth, that forgets the particularity of God's reconciling way with the world in Jesus Christ, and that fails to look for an empowering change in ourselves. This variety of unitarianism often supports a largely intellectual quest to understand the first cause and designer of the world, a quest that correlates in ethics with a commitment to universal laws of nature. Occasionally, it reduces to a virtually academic and speculative interest in religion. Today, it sometimes comes to expression in an eclectic deism that finds elements of "truth" in all traditions, but balks at the specific demands of following Jesus as well as at any talk of conversion or a change of heart.

There is also a unitarianism of the Son that forgets to engage God's dynamic power and presence in the world and also fails to look for a continuing repentance or change in ourselves. Marcion's dualism is essentially also a unitarianism of the Son. In more recent times, this sort of unitarianism has also taken pietistic and ethical forms. As pietism, it centers all loyalty, worship, and devotion on Jesus as Savior-Companion. As ethics, it supports a narrow and imitative legalism in sharply distinct communities: Jesus becomes a new law. Today the ethical form of the unitarianism of the Son sometimes issues in a superdiscipleship that fails to encourage participation in the world of commercial and civil institutions, and that underestimates inevitable corruptions in the community of disciples.

Finally, there is a unitarianism of the Spirit that fails to engage God in the world of structures and institutions, and that also leaves behind the particularity of Jesus Christ. Inner life and spirituality become the fundamental principle. The truth of God and ourselves is sought in an inward awareness, a touching of the human spirit by the divine. The usual result is a somewhat amorphous spirituality that concentrates on personal experiences of healing and renewal. Today this form of unitarianism often tends toward a therapeutic stance that views participation in relationships, communities, and institutions largely as a means to personal growth, and that reduces Jesus to a healer who makes few significant demands.

By contrast, trinitarian theology points toward the dynamic interrelation of Father, Son, and Spirit. It insists that there is no genuine response to God that does not include all three: a participatory engagement in God's world, the pattern of faithfulness embodied in Jesus Christ, and a spiritual turning, reorientation, and enlargement of the person. With these insistences, trinitarian theology both summarizes and portrays the Christian community's distinct experience of faithfulness and renewal. Trinitarian believing claims that this kind of life, rather than the forms of life supported by various unitarianisms, turns people toward God's realm and toward the true communion with God in community with others for which we have been created, sustained, and redeemed. It claims that this kind of life is genuinely responsive to the contours of God's relation to creatures.

We can put this last point another way. Trinitarian theology claims that these three things—our responsive interaction in the world, our repentant reorientation, and our discipleship—amount to integral aspects of a single dynamic or trajectory called faithfulness and new life. This is the Christian community's distinctive threefold apprehension of life-before-God, and trinitarian theology also makes the further claim that such a life responds to a single dynamic or trajectory in God's relation to creatures. In this sense, it points toward the triunity of God-before-life.[13] It intimates that our apprehensions of Father, Son, and Spirit represent discernments of a single divine reality ordering the world toward redemption.

We might take this a step further and say that the Christian community's experience of faithfulness and new life points to the reality of God beyond our experience, or the reality of God as God is apart from God's relation to creatures. As Karl Rahner put it, "The 'economic' Trinity is the 'immanent' Trinity and the 'immanent' Trinity is the 'economic' Trinity."[14] Rahner believed that, as understood by the experience of faith and the witness of scripture, Father, Son, and Spirit point toward true distinctions and interrelations within God.

Having said this, we might then add that the final reality in which we live and move and have our being is relational at its very core. This is the deep reality in, with, and under the self in its relations to others, as well as in, with, and under the being of anything in its relations with others. At a practical level, this would reinforce the participatory and relational vector of saving faith and new life, and it would offer a metaphysical ground for an ethics of interactive responsibility.

Although I favor relational portraits of life and reality, I am uncertain whether it helps to claim that God is relational "in Godself." The assumption of eternal distinctions in God (as well as the assumption that there are none) makes me theologically uneasy because it seems metaphysically excessive. For one thing, as the history of doctrine so clearly shows, the Trinity is a point at which the temptation to speculate is especially strong, but where it seems wise to philosophize no further than scripture and piety require. Moreover, the more important and practical trinitarian point is this: God, the one in whom we live and move and have our being, is relational in the sense that God is a fountain who overflows and goes out from God. The Father goes out in creating, sustaining, and redeeming creatures, in creating the world and meeting us in it at every turn. The Son reconciles persons to God and to one another in the self-emptying form of a servant who crosses boundaries and goes out to sinners. The Spirit goes out to turn, renew, and gather persons into new community. This "going-out" is God exercising God's own glory and perfection in the manifestation and communication of God to creatures.[15] This is God initiating, sustaining, and renewing the true communion with God in community with others that is God's saving purpose. Trinitarian theology affirms that the divine being, the deep reality in, with, and under both self and others, is communicative in the sense that God's disposition or propensity is toward true communion in community. This going-out is the dynamic actuality and trajectory behind and beneath all things, the encompassing and ordering reality that is more real than appearances. This is God as we experience God in the threefold economy, and this is why trinitarian theology authorizes an ethic of faithful participation that respects and furthers the good and abundant life of true communion in community.

THE GOD BEYOND

At the same time that we make this metaphysical claim (and I should like to underscore that it *is* a metaphysical claim), we should also say that the Trinity is a symbol that points to the God beyond rational concept. "God is one in essence, three in person, Father, Son, and Holy Spirit."[16] Although they often take the form of propositions such as this one, trinitarian reflections are poetic in the sense that they push beyond the competency of rational propositions. The best trinitarian thinking always returns to the early communities' exploration into their experiences of redemption, and to the pattern or economy displayed in narrative, poetic, liturgical, and homiletical literatures of the Bible. It always relies on Father, Son, and Spirit in the continuing experiences of Christian communities. Apart from these experiences it makes no sense.

Consider that John Calvin rejected as unduly speculative even Augustine's celebrated analogy between the Trinity and the faculties of understanding, will, and memory in the human soul.[17] We might say that the Trinity is a supremely "unpicturable" doctrine. Even the most able students of theology are unable to draw it. This is so because trinitarian theology finally means to point to the God who continually goes out from Godself in the exercise of God's own glory, and whose plenitude or fullness must therefore always remain a mystery. Trinitarian theology is a bit of reflective poetry that points to the God beyond our concept of God.

This antimodernist aspect of trinitarian wisdom pushes toward something more important than clear and distinct ideas. Not unlike the medieval mystic Meister Eckhart, good trinitarian thinking is finally willing to let go of our concept of God for fear that this, too, may become an idol. As all good theology must, it tries to put us in touch with that which finally remains beyond our words. It therefore has a profound self-negating dimension. It refuses to be satisfied with the God we have thought of, and it refuses to claim literal or univocal competence for itself at the price of denying God's incomprehensibility.[18] The best trinitarian thinking recognizes that our words about God are analogical and symbolic.

This does not mean that traditional trinitarian language is of little importance. We appropriately value and respect the trinitarian symbols of Father, Son, and Spirit as terms that apply to God and as terms that engage the heart of the Scriptures and the redemptive experiences of Christian communities. We value and respect them as symbols that refer to life-before-God-and-God-before-life. Yet precisely because we respect the plenitude of the divine reality to which these symbols point, we do not limit ourselves to them. We also make use of the wider symbolic treasury of the Scriptures as well as other sources of insight. Not that our words should be multiplied at random. This would lead to an abdication of our responsibility. Words need to be selected and employed in light of the "theo-logic" of Christian communities and traditions, and in ways that do not truncate the Christian community's dynamic apprehension of life-before-God-and-God-before-life. To recall an earlier point, trinitarian theologians will not use words about God that devalue creation. Neither will they employ terms that reduce the Christian life to merely therapeutic experiences of personal growth and renewal.

But this clearly is not to say that Father, Son, and Spirit are the only words that we should use to talk about God. Indeed, one way to protect against idolatry and the consequent domestication of God is to pluralize our words about God. We should observe, for example, that the exclusive use of symbols such as King, Father, and Son encourages us to adopt an exclusively male image of God. It encourages us to confuse the incomprehensible and immeasurable God with our own conceptual pictures and measures. Moreover, it clearly is the case that male images have no exclusive competence when it comes to portraying the divine going-out toward true communion in community. As Rosemary Radford Ruether suggests, the exclusive use of male images tempts us to idolatry.[19] The same may be said for the exclusive use of personal words about God, the exclusive use of nonpersonal words, and so on.

THE SENSE THE TRINITY MAKES

Trinitarian theology makes sense, not as speculative mathematics, but as a bit of faithful reflection that emerges from the Christian community's continuing exploration into God and ourselves. The best trinitarian thinking contributes to a vision that supports a particular form of life in worship and in work. It affirms that God is faithful, and it proposes that to live doxologically is to be turned from corrupting narrowness toward love of God and neighbor. Trinitarian theology expresses and interprets the apprehension of Christians and their communities that God goes out from Godself in initiating, sustaining, and renewing the true communion with God in community with others that is God's saving purpose. It therefore also indicates that to praise Father, Son, and Spirit in worship and in ethics is to embrace the good and abundant life of true communion with God in community.

But it is important to remember that trinitarian theology makes this sense as a faithful reflection that does not claim to capture or fully comprehend God and God's glory. The Trinity makes sense as it endeavors to point beyond itself toward the mysterious reality to whom we stand related in all of our many relations. It contributes to wisdom only when it does not degenerate into a mere orthodoxy, a dead letter, or an idol to be promulgated as unchangeable, unquestionable, and univocal dogma. Trinitarian theology serves genuine piety and faithfulness as it continues an exploration into God and ourselves.

4 Meaning and Mystery of Resurrection

An article in *Newsweek* for Easter, 1996, noted that 87 percent of Americans say they believe that Jesus was raised from the dead, although many remain uncertain of how to understand their belief.[1] It also noted that scholars offer vastly different theories of what happened. Some insist that Jesus' physical body was raised. One argues that it rotted away in the tomb, while another suggests that it was eaten by wild dogs. An Australian writer says that Jesus was administered a slow-acting poison but was later revived. A number of Bible scholars and theologians maintain that resurrection faith emerged when, after his death, followers continued to experience Jesus Christ as the living Lord of their lives. Others believe that what was raised was Jesus' transformed or glorified body, but they differ over whether the body was physical.[2]

This chapter is a theological meditation on the meaning and truth of Jesus' resurrection. I suggest that Jesus' resurrection should be understood in the context of two broader and interrelated patterns. The first is the pattern of the Christ event, and it also includes Jesus' life, ministry, and death. The second is the wider framework of creation, sin, providence, and redemption, and what these symbols say about God and ourselves. When understood in these contexts, I believe that Jesus' resurrection attests to Jesus' way in the world, and that it lifts up Jesus Christ as living Lord of our continuing life. It also indicates that God is faithful, and it points to the new and true life of God's coming reign as the possibility and destiny of human life.

I, too, shall turn to the much discussed question of what happened, but only after I have outlined these meanings and claims of resurrection faith. This is because I am convinced that the knot of beliefs about Jesus Christ, God, and humanity that is associated with Jesus' resurrection is not exhausted by any historical reconstruction. Indeed, so far as the fundamental theology is concerned, we can be comfortable with any understanding of what happened that witnesses to the central meanings and claims of resurrection faith.

RESURRECTION FAITH

For Christian believing, Jesus' resurrection is part of a larger pattern. It cannot be appropriately understood apart from the story of his life, ministry, and death. Neither can it be appropriately apprehended apart from the wider framework of creation, sin, providence, and redemption.

Indeed, when we isolate Jesus' resurrection from the broader context of his life, ministry, and death, we misunderstand it and distort it. Resurrection then appears to be an emblem of redemption apart from mission, apart from discipleship, and without cost. It then becomes a symbol of untroubled fulfillment. Similarly, when we separate Jesus' resurrection from the broader context of creation, sin, providence, and redemption, we forget its place within the larger drama of God and ourselves. Then we simply regard it as an isolated and unexpected occurrence. We fail to discern that Jesus' resurrection points beyond itself, that it intimates the otherness that encompasses our lives, and that it testifies to the steadfast faithfulness of the God who does not abandon sinful and wayward creatures. We forget that, by the grace of God and despite sin's persistent corruption, resurrection is an emblem of human possibility and destiny.

These observations bring us to an initial meaning of Jesus' resurrection that cannot be repeated often enough in a culture of feel-good religion and cheap grace where a gospel of success and easy fulfillment too often reigns supreme. Although one rarely hears it said in our prosperous society, *God's raising of Jesus from the dead lifts up the way of the cross.* Jesus' resurrection is God's "yes" to a manner of living oriented by love of God and neighbor even to the point of confrontation with powers that be. His resurrection lifts up Jesus' costly ministry of reconciliation and calls us to follow. Resurrection faith claims that Jesus' way in the world, this costly way of reconciliation, summarizes and embodies the pattern of good and abundant life for which we have been fitted and sustained all along. It points to his passionate way with the world, his living-for-others, as the revelation of God's way with the world.

We may go a step further and say that Jesus Christ embodies true communion with God in community with others, and he therefore represents the reversal of sin's narrowing and diminution of the life that befits us. Human beings are equipped to be faithful and creative participants; we are fitted for covenantal relationships of attentiveness, fidelity, and responsibility with God and with others. Sin means that, although we are created for this good and abundant life, we are chronically confused, misoriented, and misdirected in the ways in which we live and move and deploy our powers. We are in the grips of a corrupting tendency, an impeding influence that alienates us from God and from others. Sin means the way toward *death,* or as Gustavo Gutiérrez puts it, sin is a "breach of friendship with God and others" that invites enmity and division.[3] Sin's corruption entails the constriction of human vision, commitment, and responsibility as well as a consequent shrinking or recession from the community of all things in their mutual interdependence and dependence on God.[4]

Jesus' resurrection indicates that his way in the world, the way that leads to his crucifixion, is the efficacious way toward *life,* the way toward renewed vision, commitment, and responsibility. It therefore calls us to the way of interrelation with God and neighbor that crosses barriers and boundaries. It proclaims that this is the way toward the enlargement of persons, toward genuine and faithful participation in God's world. Jesus' resurrection helps us to see that "What has come into being in him was life, and the life was the light of all people"(John 1:3b–4).

Or, again, we may say that God's way with the world in Jesus Christ is the way of new community overcoming division. Therefore, the one who embodies the way of the cross is also the one who both teaches and embodies love of God and neighbor and even love of enemies. He announces and embodies the coming reign of God. He eats with outcasts, tax collectors, and sinners. He welcomes children. He heals the sick. His way with the world is like the Lord's Supper—a lost nearness restored, a banquet to which all are invited and at which all may be nourished. His is the way of community for all, most especially the marginal and oppressed who so often are excluded. This is the way in life that we are called to walk. This is the particular pattern in life that is lifted up, and this is why resurrection faith so often makes for tension with established powers and practices.

"And remember, I am with you always, to the end of the age" (Matt. 28:20). *For Christian believing, Jesus' resurrection not only lifts up Jesus' way with the world, it also attests to his continuing presence.* Here, again, we should insist on an indissoluble interconnection among Jesus' resurrection, the pattern and form of his life, ministry, and death, and the broader sweep of God's dealings with the world from creation to coming reign. Indeed, the fuller meaning of his continuing presence becomes apparent only when we outline who Jesus Christ is, only when we summarize the pattern of what he says, does, and endures, and we are able to do this only when we interpret Jesus in context.

Jesus Christ is not just anyone. For one thing, he is rabbi and prophet. In word and in deed, he teaches the truth about life and justice and love, about the world as God's commonwealth of grace, and about the coming reign of judgment and promise. Jesus Christ is king, the governor who rules over and guides the Christian life, because he pioneers and embodies a way in life that accords with the truth. Oriented by devotion to God, he embodies a way that calls the misdirected to repentance, restrains the use of force, insists on fairness and mercy, cares for the poor, and engenders and requires attentiveness to the needs and interests of others. Or, again, borrowing images from the book of Hebrews, Jesus Christ is high priest and perfect sacrifice. He empowers true life because he imparts the power of God that turns people from sin and sets them on the way toward the kingdom of true communion in community. Jesus Christ is the great occasion of tragic and innocent suffering, the cruciform power of repentance who punctuates and underscores and will not let us turn our gaze from the sight of sin's tragic consequences. To all but the hardest of hearts, this is the power of God to change hearts.

It follows, then, that God's raising of Jesus does not mean the emergence of a vague salvific presence in the life of the Christian community. Instead, it means the continuing presence of God's way with humanity in the particular person of Jesus Christ and what he says, does, and endures. It means the continuing presence of the prophet, pioneer, and priest. By his resurrection, Jesus Christ becomes the teacher who continues to instruct, the leader who continues to guide, and the power who continues to empower. He becomes the living Lord of reconciliation and renewal who is still with us.[5]

"And remember, I am with you always, to the end of the age." Just because this final sentence of Matthew's Gospel points to the continuing presence of Jesus Christ, it communicates both the authority and the promise of Jesus' sovereignty. It indicates, on the one hand, that we never escape the government of Jesus Christ, the one who teaches the truth, embodies the way, and empowers the life. Although we sometimes forget him and deny him, he does not forget us. Although we travel at a great distance from him in time, we do not escape his claim on us. That Jesus is Lord means that we are not our own.

"And remember, I am with you always, to the end of the age." The promise in these words is that, when it comes to the ministry of reconciliation, the labor of new and renewed communion and community in the tragic absence of communion in community and in the dispiriting presence of struggle, emptiness, and division, we are not alone. In the language of the Heidelberg Catechism, we belong to our faithful savior.[6] True, we are sent on a plainly revolutionary mission to gather a single people from among the world's divided peoples, to gather one genuine and faithful community from among the world's divided nations. But when it comes to this world-transforming mission, this project against long odds, we are not left to our own devices. Resurrection faith claims that Jesus the Christ—the one who teaches the truth, embodies the way, and empowers the life—remains the risen Lord of the Christian community's continuing life in the world.

This brings us to a third important meaning of Jesus' resurrection: *it makes a claim about God-before-life, about the Holy One with whom we deal in all of our many dealings.* It points to a meaning, purpose, and direction of God's encompassing presence. God does not abandon to destruction the one who teaches the truth, embodies the way, and empowers the life. God does not leave us without a savior who continues to be the way toward the good and abundant life of God's reign. Jesus' resurrection therefore indicates that the great God of glory, the One who creates and sustains all things, is also the good God of grace, the One who redeems. God is not loveless, faithless power. God is faithful. God is good. We depend on God for existence and for life, but also for new life. This is why all persons and animals and plants and things belong to God. This is why history is never apart from redemptive possibility, why it is not only the history of sin, suffering, love, repentance, and mission, but also the history of faith as a gift of God and as the power of God to renew.

In Calvin's vocabulary, this is knowledge of God the redeemer.[7] It is knowledge of God's benevolence, an apprehension that supports a sublime and practical confidence. Even in the face of suffering, death, decay, and destruction, those who commit themselves to *life* and to true communion in community, those who participate faithfully in God's world, gain courage and strength from the conviction that the sovereign God is faithful.

The core affirmation is as old as Christian community itself.

> For I am convinced that neither death, nor life, nor angels, nor rulers, nor things present, nor things to come, nor powers, nor height, nor depth, nor anything else in all creation, will be able to separate us from the love of God in Christ Jesus our Lord (Rom. 8:38–39).

As the Puritan theologian Jonathan Edwards put it, redemption is God's greatest work, and the basis for redemption is "the constancy and perpetuity of God's mercy and faithfulness."[8] This is the final reality on which we can rely.

Such "cosmic optimism" has never been easy to sustain.[9] On the one hand, we seem constantly in danger of transmuting it into a guarantee of all of our needs, wants, and desires. The history of the Christian movement is therefore littered with pious insistences that the truly righteous cannot suffer, that God will protect and advance Christian nations and empires, that the faithful will be granted material wealth, and so on. Too often, we fasten on symbols of divine benevolence and redemption without remembering that the new life they promise is a passionate devotion to God and others that entails a displacement of our isolated interests. This is another reason why a theology of resurrection ought not be separated from the way of the cross.

Then again, in a world of fragmentation and conflict, not only we ourselves and all of our attempts at restraining evil and pursuing good, but also the dynamic movement and cause of God's reign itself, are assailed and deflected on all sides. In Samaria or in Bosnia, in Greensville or in Richmond, altogether too great a share of present reality is defined by violence, starvation, and disease, by airstrikes and burning villages, by deterioration and despair, and by prison riots and record-breaking murder counts. This is why a deep practical and existential issue for created, dependent, and contingent human beings has to do with the relations of power and goodness. This is why a primary point for piety, for the heart of passionate believing and identity, concerns the trustworthiness, dependability, and sovereignty of God. H. Richard Niebuhr put it this way.

> The great anxiety of life, the great distrust, appears in the doubt that the Power whence all things come, the Power which has thrown the self and its companions into existence, is not good. The question is always before us, Is Power good? Is it good to and for what it has brought into being? Is it good with the goodness of integrity? Is it good as adorable and delightful? . . . But our second great problem is whether it is not forever defeated in actual existence by loveless, thoughtless power. The resurrection of Jesus Christ in power, is at one and the same time the demonstration of the power of goodness and the goodness of power.[10]

Resurrection faith affirms that God is good and God is great.

Finally, there is yet another meaning of Jesus' resurrection: *it intimates destiny.* It testifies that, as the purpose of God is to empower true, good, renewed, and abundant life, so our own chief possibility and end is not death and destruction but true, good, renewed, and abundant life. Here again, we come across an important affirmation for a Christian interpretation of history. Together with the creation symbol, resurrection points to the meaningfulness of history as an event of divine faithfulness and goodness. Together with other symbols of redemption, it points to the transformation of history and of fragmented, misoriented, misdirected, and corrupted life by regenerative possibility. Resurrection tells us, in the language of the Westminster Shorter Catechism, that the chief end and destiny of human being is to glorify God and enjoy God forever.[11]

Or again, Edwards once wrote, in commentary on 1 Corinthians 13:8–10, that heaven is a world of mutual love.[12] For the Puritan pastor, people are made to live "in the presence of the eternal, unending absolute glory, to participate in the celebration of cosmic deliverance."[13] We might say that people are created, sustained, and redeemed for this: true communion with God in community with others. Resurrection faith claims that the meaning of history as well as the chief end and destiny of human being is the kingdom of God.

WHAT HAPPENED?

With this in mind, let us now turn to a question that has received so much discussion. What happened following Jesus' crucifixion? Here, it is important to get a few things straight at the start.

None of the four Gospels depicts anyone witnessing the resurrection event. Instead, emphasis falls on the appearances of the risen Christ and those who witnessed them. All four Gospels contain the tradition about the empty tomb (although it does not appear in Paul's letters). Apart from this, however, there is a noteworthy lack of concord. Indeed, rather than a continuous account of the appearances of the risen Christ, we find relatively independent stories that are often placed into somewhat disjointed narrative contexts.[14]

The stories were not standardized, and they do not paint an entirely consistent picture of the way in which people experienced the presence of the resurrected one. They flicker and wobble. For example, Matthew 28 says that Jesus appeared to "Mary Magdalene and the other Mary" just after they left the tomb, and that the two women "took hold of his feet, and worshipped him." It also says that when the eleven disciples saw the risen Jesus at Galilee "they worshipped him; but some doubted." The longer ending to the Gospel of Mark says that Jesus appeared to Mary Magdalene outside of the tomb. She told others that he was alive, but they did not believe. Then "he appeared in another form" to two of those to whom Mary had spoken. In Luke 24, the risen Christ breaks bread with disciples and then vanishes from their sight. In John 20, Mary Magdalene at first has trouble recognizing the risen Christ outside of the tomb. Other appearances in the same chapter have Jesus entering into a locked house, but also Thomas touching Jesus' hands and sides.

Statements about Paul's experiences of the risen Christ deserve special mention. According to Acts 9, 22, and 26, Paul saw a great light and heard Jesus' voice on the Damascus road. Depending on what is meant by statements that Jesus "appeared" to Paul in Acts 9:17 and 26:16 (and also 1 Corinthians 15:8), Paul may also have seen the risen Christ. The experiences of those traveling with Paul are unevenly portrayed. They hear the voice but see no one in Acts 9. In Acts 22, they see the light but do not hear the voice, and they fall to the ground with Paul in Acts 26.

Some of Paul's most important remarks about resurrection come in 1 Corinthians 15, where he also summarizes the tradition that he received concerning Christ's death, resurrection, and appearances. Here, the apostle links Christ's resurrection with the resurrection of the dead: "Christ has been raised from the dead, the first fruits of those who have died" (15:20). He also confronts some critical questions. "But someone will ask, 'How are the dead raised? With what kind of body do they come?'" (15:35).

Paul's response centers on a rather complex seed image. He says that seeds do not come to life without first dying in the ground. And, the seed that one sows is not "the body that is to be, but a bare seed, perhaps of wheat or of some other grain. But God gives it a body as he has chosen, and to each kind of seed its own body" (15:37–38). Similarly, says the apostle, there are different sorts of flesh for humans, animals, birds, and fish. And in addition to earthly bodies, there are also heavenly bodies, such as the sun, moon, and stars. The heavenly ones have one sort of glory or luster, the earthly ones another, and the glories of each heavenly body also are distinct.

Then comes the theological application. "So it is with the resurrection of the dead. What is sown is perishable, what is raised is imperishable" (15:42). That is, the earthly, biological body and the resurrected body are not the same. Says the most poetic of apostles, "It is sown a physical body, it is raised a spiritual body (*soma pneumatikon*)" (15:44). Paul aligns the former with the first Adam who was from the dust of the earth, and the second with Christ or the last Adam who is from heaven. Thus, "flesh and blood cannot inherit the kingdom of God, nor does the perishable inherit the imperishable" (15:50). Here is a great mystery: "we will all be changed" (15:51).

A somewhat different focus prevails in Romans 6–8, where Paul aligns resurrection with the rebirth of the person, the new life that has already begun with baptism. "We have been buried with him by baptism into death, so that, just as Christ was raised from the dead by the glory of the Father, so we too might walk in newness of life" (Rom. 6:4). The emphasis falls on a reshaping of persons, a quality of life, a new vitality and living to God into which Christ introduces Christians. By his resurrection, Christ has become the first fruits of a new mode of life, and the result is that human beings can now live in a new way of the Spirit.

But, as Carolyn Walker Bynum points out, in 1 Corinthians 15, "the image of the seed is an image of radical transformation." Although it points to a measure of continuity with present life, emphasis falls on the relation between Jesus' resurrection and the resurrection of the dead, on a change from the perishable to the imperishable. Moreover, the precise nature of the change that Paul has in mind remains enigmatic, and the expression "spiritual body" seems something of an oxymoron—perhaps even an intentionally broken image.[15]

One might argue that we cannot move from 1 Corinthians 15 to a discussion of Jesus' resurrection, because Paul is here discussing the more general resurrection of the dead. But this argument comes to grief over Paul's own insistence on the close link between the two. Again, in verses 45 to 49, he associates Jesus Christ, the "man of heaven," with the body that is imperishable rather than perishable and spiritual rather than physical. It therefore seems that, when we consider Paul's understanding of resurrection, whether Jesus' or our own, we must reckon not only with a new quality of living but also with some significant discontinuity between physical, earthly bodies and resurrected bodies. We need to puzzle over a mystery.

SOME RECENT INTERPRETATIONS

Karl Barth approached the matter this way. He affirmed that Jesus was physically raised, but he also claimed that the New Testament stories of Jesus' resurrection are imaginative and poetic and marked by a kind of obscurity. "For they are describing an event beyond the reaches of historical research or depiction." Again, Barth insisted on the importance of the empty tomb and the ascension, although he noted that they are presupposed and hinted at rather than referred to explicitly in the later apostolic preaching. "Even in the Easter narratives," he wrote, they are indicated rather than described, and "in the strict sense the ascension occurs only in Acts 1:9f." Barth continued,

> there are reasons for this. The content of the Easter witness, the Easter event was not that the disciples found the tomb empty or that they saw Him go up to heaven, but that when they had lost Him through death they were sought and found by Him as the Resurrected.[16]

Emil Brunner, another Swiss Reformed theologian, claimed that Christians believe in the risen Christ, "not because the Resurrection is told as a narrative of something that happened," but because they know Christ as living and present.[17]

> Hence all questions of "how" and "where" the Resurrection took place, including the question of the Empty Tomb and the physical resurrection understood in this sense, are secondary. This is so because we who, in view of our own resurrection, are called "His brethren," among whom He is the First-born, do not believe in our physical resurrection in the sense of an empty tomb. Here again we see the significance of the original Pauline account of the Res-

> urrection. Just as Paul lays no stress upon the Empty Tomb, so on the other hand, he lays decisive emphasis upon the parallels between the Resurrection of Jesus and our own. . . . Even if Paul (which we simply do not know) did know anything about the Empty Tomb, it was not for him a fact of central importance, because for us there will not be an empty grave.[18]

Brunner went on to say that Paul's teaching about a spiritual body fits uneasily if at all with the medieval idea of the opening of graves on the last day. And, he concluded

> Resurrection of the body, yes; Resurrection of the *flesh,* no! The "Resurrection of the body" does not mean the identity of the resurrection body with the material (although already transformed) body of flesh; but the resurrection of the body means the continuity of the individual personality on this side, and on that, of death.[19]

Rudolf Bultmann, the controversial advocate of demythologizing the Christian message, claimed that the cross and the resurrection are inseparably united, and that they are made present through preaching. Indeed, the living Jesus "comes again; he always comes again" in the proclamation.[20] *"Faith in the resurrection is really the same thing as faith in the saving efficacy of the cross."*[21] And, we come to believe in this saving efficacy because Christ meets us in the word of preaching. That is why resurrection faith is not tied to the results of historical research into past events.

> The real Easter faith is faith in the word of preaching which brings illumination. If the event of Easter Day is in any sense an historical event additional to the event of the cross, it is nothing else than the rise of faith in the risen Lord. . . . The resurrection itself is not an event of past history. All that historical criticism can establish is the fact that the first disciples came to believe in the resurrection.[22]

Somewhat similarly, Willi Marxsen claimed that "The declaration that Jesus has risen came to be made" as "an inference derived from personal faith." Thus, the words "Jesus is risen" essentially mean that "the cause of Jesus continues, or in the words of the hymn, 'still he comes today.'"[23] Years ago, Peter C. Hodgson accepted the basic outlines of Marxsen's interpretation and said that the resurrection "is an inference from a present experience to a past occasion for this experience." It "is an historic event in its present modality, not as an historically observable past event."[24] More recently, he has written that Jesus' resurrection is Jesus' arising to action and coming to stand in the world as "the agent or representative of God engaged in a work of reconciliatory emancipation." Jesus' resurrection means that Jesus is spiritually present to the Christian community as the companion who reconstructs our broken faith, and it also indicates that our self-identity after death is preserved "by participation in a community or a spiritual realm of being."[25]

Some other positions may be understood as variations on those I have mentioned. For example, Stephen T. Davis holds that the empty tomb is crucial, and that Jesus' resurrection is a matter of bodily transformation. Jesus' resurrection body, says Davis, "was physical (i.e., it took up space, could be located, could be seen under right conditions, etc.) but also in some sense supernatural (which accounts for the 'spiritual' motifs in Paul and some of the appearance stories in the Gospels)."[26] By contrast, John Shelby Spong suggests that Simon Peter had a "vision of Jesus alive" as much as six months after Jesus' death and crucifixion. The vision occurred in Galilee, where Simon witnessed to other disciples who also saw Jesus risen. This is the experience behind the resurrection idea. At the time of the Feast of Tabernacles, they gathered in Jerusalem to share their faith, and so the story of Easter unfolded in this context. Thus, writes Spong, "the truth of Jesus alive and available created the narratives and the legends."[27]

John Hick writes that

> the term "resurrection" has been used throughout Christian history to refer to the transitional event or events in virtue of which the Jesus movement survived the death of its founder. . . . Precisely what this transitional event was we cannot now discern with confidence.[28]

Hick's "preferred conjecture" is that "there was some kind of experience of seeing Jesus after his death, an appearance or appearances which came to be known as his resurrection."[29] Early Christians had inner spiritual experiences similar to Paul's on the Damascus road as presented in Acts 9, 22, and 26.[30]

My own understanding (if "understanding" is the right word) is that, when they had lost him through crucifixion and death, the disciples encountered the deep strangeness of grace in Jesus' presence after his earthly presentness. Jesus still came to the disciples as the one who instructs, leads, and delivers. The dwelling of Christ with and in the disciples, this incursion, is what gathered them together as the members of his body in the world. This mystical union, as we might (inadequately) call it, is the reality that lies behind the resurrection narratives of the New Testament.[31] It also continues to characterize the faithful experiences of Christian communities. In preaching, sacrament, and common life, Jesus Christ is spiritually and really present to Christians as the one who continues to teach the truth, embody the way, and empower the life.

A PRIMARY QUESTION

Having surveyed these interpretations of what happened, we might very well ask a number of questions. What counts as evidence for and against one or another position? Which positions seem plausible in the light of contemporary biology? How do the several interpretations relate to philosophical reflections about mind, body, and personal identity? How do they accord with one or another ecclesiastical standard? All of these questions and more are important, and were I to develop an exhaustive theology of resurrection, I would need to say how my particular understanding of what happened takes them into account. Theologically considered, however, a primary question is simply this. Does a particular interpretation of what happened testify to the central meanings and claims of resurrection faith?

Welcome interpretations of what happened witness to the lifting up of Jesus' way with the world. They support the claim that Jesus' manner of living marks off the pattern of good and abundant life for which we humans are fitted and sustained. Theologically cordial interpretations of what happened also intimate Jesus' continuing presence; they uphold the claim that Jesus Christ continues to teach, lead, and empower. Again, theologically welcome interpretations of what happened witness to the faithfulness of God, and so contribute to the conviction that God is great and God is good. Finally, they also testify that the purpose of God is to empower true, good, and abundant life. They contribute to the suggestion that the meaning of history as well as the chief possibility and end of human being is the coming reign of God.

I think that this standard can be met by interpretations of what happened ranging from Barth's insistence on a physical event, to Davis's conception of a resurrection body that is both physical and supernatural, to Brunner's ruminations about personality, to Hodgson's notion of spiritual presence, to Bultmann's understanding of the coming of Jesus in the preached word, to Spong's claims for the emergence of the vision of Jesus alive, to Hick's conjecture concerning a spiritual experience similar to Paul's on the Damascus road.[32] Nonetheless, the range is not unlimited. There are possible interpretations of what happened that do not meet the standard.

For example, claims that the disciples experienced an inchoate spirit of life and reassurance, and that people today continue to have similar experiences, do not testify to God's lifting up of the way of the cross. Neither do they witness to the continuing presence of the particular person who teaches the truth, embodies the way, and empowers the life. Again, claims that Jesus only appeared to die but continued to live for some years with his disciples also do not meet the standard. Neither do bald statements that Jesus' body rotted away in the tomb. Neither does the claim that Jesus' physical body was resuscitated and that he interacted for a time with early disciples. These statements do not meet the standard because they fail to include an interpretation of Jesus' continuing presence that connects with other claims and meanings of resurrection faith, such as the convictions that God is faithful and that the new and true life of God's reign is the chief possibility and destiny of human being.

One of my purposes in interpreting resurrection, its meaning, and its truth in this manner is to maximize possibilities for faithful interpretation by recognizing that we need not say one and only one thing about what happened. I think that this maximization reflects the varied witnesses presented in the New Testament literature as well as the dynamic character of the resurrection mystery. Pastorally speaking, I also believe that it communicates a word of grace to troubled souls who may have the impression that they must affirm one or another thing about resurrected bodies in order to be Christian, or saved, or faithful. A friend at Bunker Hill Presbyterian Church may believe that the message of new and true life is tied to Jesus' resurrection as a physical bodily occurrence. A member of the Vanguard class in Richmond may have something more like Brunner's or Hodgson's position in mind. Or, again, a good and faithful Christian may admit that she or he is simply unsure of how to conceive it.

Clearly, one may raise significant questions about each of these positions. None escapes all difficulties. But perhaps we should expect this. After all, as the apostle Paul well knew, our theologies of resurrection can only be attempts to point toward a mystery that we do not fully comprehend. Inspired (we hope) by grace, they try to express and to put us in touch with that which transcends the sayable. My point is simply that, as we now see through a glass darkly, any and all interpretations of what happened are welcome so long as they testify to central meanings and claims of resurrection faith.

IN LIFE AND DEATH

The meaning of Jesus' resurrection is that "in life and death, we belong to God,"[33] that God is not absent and that therefore we are not separated. We belong to God in life. We are called to live a capacious, good, and abundant life of true communion with God in community with others, rather than a narrowed or imploded life of simply "looking out for number one." We are called to seek the good of our neighbor, to attend not only to our own interests but also to the interests of others (1 Cor. 10:24; Phil. 2:4). We are called to be disciples of Jesus Christ, to risk living and walking in his way, the way that God has lifted up. We are claimed for faithful obedience by the living Lord who continues to instruct, guide, and empower. We are not our own, and we are not alone. We are called to a revolutionary ministry of reconciliation in the continuing presence of the Lord of reconciliation and renewal.

This is not all. That we belong to God in life also means that we are renewed and enabled to live in this way and to pursue this ministry by the confident conviction that the power who creates and bears all things (stars and worlds, universes seen and unseen) is good. The power of reality and being who upholds all things is redeemer. Therefore, by the grace of God-in-Christ, and no matter how skewed, destructive, and terrifying it becomes, history is never separated from regenerative possibility. This is another reason not to skip over the cross and the crucifixion. Even where God is withdrawn, there remains a density and an enigma of possibility, and in this sense, human life and history are never apart from the miracle of saving grace. Therefore, you and I are freed from our fundamental anxiety, and we are enabled to relinquish a narrowing life of defensive implosion. The conviction that the point of life is not death but new life and true life frees us from tortured commitments to our own isolated advantage as well as from futile attempts to defend ourselves against the forces of decline, decay, and destruction. It enables us to take up a life of capacious attention to and faithful participation in God's all-inclusive commonwealth of grace. It lends us the courage to pursue a ministry of reconciliation in the face of long odds and tragic suffering.

And, finally, we belong to God in death. The great God of glory is the good God of grace. God is faithful. The power who bears all things in nature and in history destroys only to reestablish and renew. This is why the apostle is quite correct to say that "whether we live or whether we die, we are the Lord's" (Romans 14:8). Resurrection faith means that, as we may live in nondefensive confidence, so we may also die in the confidence that God-in-Christ is faithful, and that the chief end of human being is to glorify God and enjoy God forever.

Christianity may be understood as a symbol system, a configuration or a cycle of symbols, that offers a profoundly true account of God and ourselves. On this view, like creation, sin, providence, incarnation, and kingdom, resurrection is a basic symbol of the Christian framework. To say this does not beg the question of its historical actuality. True symbols often emerge in interconnection with history and fact. Nonetheless, their meaning and truth are not exhausted by these interconnections. The reason is that their symbolic patterns transgress and shatter the boundaries of past occurrence as they illuminate the enduring reality of life-before-God-and-God-before-life. The reason is that they refuse the reductive analytic-empirical and linguistic criteria of constraint that characterize too much modern thinking and that would separate us from what can shine through the everyday and the mundane. Thus, while we appropriately offer interpretations of what happened, the meaning and truth of the resurrection symbol is neither comprehended nor contained in *the right* historical reconstruction.

The resurrection symbol intimates an answer for those for whom life too often grows distant, shallow, threatening, chaotic, impenetrable, death-dealing, panicked, flattened, and reduced. It intimates an answer by intimating at least the following about life-before-God-and-God-before-life. God exalts Jesus' way in the world, a way that marks off the good and abundant life of communion in community for which we are fitted and sustained. Jesus Christ is the living Lord of the Christian community's continuing life and experience. God is faithful and God is great. The chief possibility and destiny of human life is the new and true life of God's kingdom.

The truth is that, after the disciples had lost him through crucifixion and death, these truths were lifted up when Jesus still came to them and when they encountered him as the teacher who continues to instruct, the leader who continues to guide, and the power who continues to empower. The truth is that, by raising Jesus from the dead, God gracefully lifted up God's saving way with the world.

5 Table Conversation

An ecumenical theology is capacious, generous, and open rather than narrow, stingy, and closed. It crosses barriers and boundaries in order to manifest unity, and it remains dissatisfied with isolated confessions among divided churches. In Christ, a truly ecumenical theology engages the entire inhabited world. Moreover, a strong case may be made that only such a theology will adequately address our current circumstance: you and I inhabit an interdependent world where historically distinct communions and communities routinely find themselves interacting whether they especially want to or not. The fates of many are increasingly in the hands of many. Providentially and rightly, our contemporary situation calls for capacious theologies that cross boundaries and reach out toward the *oikoumene.*

I accept this case, believing that, in our present world, narrowly confessional theologies are badly out of place. However, I also believe that the dynamic spirit of the Reformed Christian subtradition is still worth explicating, promoting, deepening, and extending. I want to have it both ways. Accordingly, my intention here is to consider the contemporary ecumenical relevance of a musty, old Calvinist idea about incarnation. But be forewarned. I will not simply repeat the old idea. I shall try to show how it may inspire us to address our present world in ways that few old Calvinists could have anticipated.

AN EARLY PROTESTANT DEBATE

We begin with a conversation at the Lord's Table. During the sixteenth century, Ulrich Zwingli, a radical critic of the Roman mass, rejected the idea of a sacramental eating, claiming that Christ's finite physical body is at the right hand of God and that it cannot be elsewhere. He proposed instead that the sacramental meal is a remembrance or commemoration of Christ's death among those who believe themselves to be reconciled to God.[1] Martin Luther held to a literal interpretation of Christ's words of institution, *Hoc est corpus meum* ("This is my body"). He assailed "the fanatics" who "follow the fancy of reason" and so find it "altogether absurd to believe that we should eat Christ's body and blood physically in the Supper."[2] Luther agreed with the Zwinglians that Christ's body is ascended to heaven and on the right hand of God. However, he argued that God's right hand signifies the divine majesty and power that is everywhere present, including "in the bread and wine at table." And, he concluded that "where the right hand of God is, there Christ's body and blood must be."[3]

John Calvin's understanding of the Eucharist, although sometimes lumped together with Zwingli's, was different still. Calvin held that Christ's body is given by the mysterious operation of the Spirit, but that it is not locally present or contained within the bread and wine. Although Christ's ascended body remains subject to the common limits of a human body, and is not in the bread but in heaven, the Supper is more than a remembrance. We are spiritually nourished in the sacramental eating. For Calvin, the real presence of Christ's body is its mystical presence in power and efficacy. The bread and wine are not vessels that contain Christ's body, but visible signs that can neither be divorced from nor equated with the mystery they signify.[4]

The understandings of the sacrament proposed by Luther and Calvin correlated with characteristically different understandings of the incarnation. For example, the Lutheran theologian Martin Chemnitz (1522–1586) claimed that, by virtue of the hypostatic union, the divine majesty (certain attributes of the divine nature, including omnipotence, omniscience, and ubiquity) was communicated to the human nature. He therefore maintained that, as of the incarnation, the body or flesh of Christ is present whenever, wherever, and however Christ wills it to be.[5] The Formula of Concord (1577) largely followed Chemnitz on this point, claiming that Christ did not always disclose his majesty during his earthly humiliation, but that now, having entered into glory, "not only as God, but also as man, he knows all things, can do all things, [and] is present to all creatures."[6]

By contrast, the Reformed scholastic Frances Turretin (1623–1687) explained that attributes of the divine nature and the human nature were both communicated to Christ's person. However, divine properties such as ubiquity, omniscience, omnipotence, and the power of making alive were not transfused into the human nature of Christ; neither were properties of the flesh communicated to the Logos. For this would have resulted in a leveling of the two natures, and a consequent destruction of Christ's genuinely finite humanity as well as his infinite deity. The Logos, Turretin wrote, is indeed united with humanity and the flesh. Being infinite, however, it is neither circumscribed nor encompassed by human nature and the flesh.[7]

THE EXTRA CALVINISTICUM

The heart of the matter is a disagreement over how the Word became flesh. Luther emphasized "the incarnate God" who is entirely defined in Jesus Christ, and he maintained that Word and flesh are so united that, as of the incarnation, the eternal Son or Logos is never apart from the flesh.[8] Calvin explained his own position this way.

> They thrust upon us as something absurd the fact that if the Word became flesh, then he was confined within the narrow prison of the earthly body. This is mere impudence! For even if the Word in his immeasurable essence united with the nature of man into one person, we do not imagine that he was confined therein. Here is something marvelous: the Son of God descended from heaven in such a way that, without leaving heaven, he willed to be

> borne in the virgin's womb, to go about the earth, and to hang upon the cross; yet he continuously filled the world even as he had done from the beginning![9]

Thus, Calvin affirmed that God the Son is manifest in the man Jesus, but not encompassed by the man Jesus. The Word became flesh and dwelt among us, and yet the Word also continues its active reign beyond the flesh. This is what Lutheran theologians called the *extra calvinisticum:* the doctrine that, both during and after the incarnation, the eternal Son, Logos, or second person of the Trinity continues his operations also beyond the flesh (*etiam extra carnem*).[10]

Over the centuries, controversy associated with the *extra calvinisticum* has generated rather serious charges. Lutherans have claimed that the Reformed separate Christ's two natures and therefore lapse into a heretical, Nestorian understanding of Christ's person. Reformed theologians have asserted that Lutherans mix or confuse Christ's two natures. The Lutherans therefore fall into the error of Eutyches, who affirmed one nature of the Word incarnate, and they also harbor Docetic tendencies toward the denial of Christ's genuine humanity. In short, each side has accused the other of failing to uphold Chalcedonian orthodoxy and therefore failing to affirm a true incarnation.[11]

Moreover, beneath the doctrinal dispute, there lies an important difference in piety or Christian experience. The Lutheran emphasis falls on the love of God the Son in making humanity its own and, indeed, fashioning a new humanity in Christ. The Reformed emphasis falls on reverence for the redeeming manifestation of the God who rules all things. In a sentence that may continue the history of Lutheran-Reformed polemics even as it also helps to explain it, Heiko Oberman observes that "With Luther the Christmas joy is more abundant, because in Christ God has fulfilled all of his promises and revealed his very being."[12] Calvin believes that, in Jesus Christ our sure redeemer, God is truly manifest in the flesh (1 Tim. 3:16), and yet he also senses that immeasurable depths of God's omnipotent reign remain hidden and unknown.[13]

THE INTRA-EXTRA DIALECTIC

It is not unusual to read that Reformed Christology is governed by the rational principle that the finite cannot contain the infinite (*finitum non capax infiniti*).[14] The expression does not occur in Calvin, however, and in the light of Calvin's interest in affirming a true incarnation, Oberman thinks we should reject it in favor of the inverse: *infinitum capax finiti.*[15] This proposal has the virtue of emphasizing a central affirmation: the infinite God really is manifest in the man Jesus. Unfortunately, it neglects the fact that, for both Calvin and other Reformed theologians, the infinite Logos cannot be limited by finite human nature and any entire inclusion of the Logos in the man Jesus also compromises his finite humanity.

Karl Barth is right, I think, to keep the broader doctrine in view. The Reformed *extra,* he reminds us, is always an *etiam extra* (an also *extra*). Along with the *extra,* Reformed theologians also asserted the *intra.* They affirmed the Logos in the flesh, although they did not want the reality of the Logos beyond the flesh abolished or suppressed. Indeed, says Barth, the formulation of the scholastic Maresius says it all: "Thus the Logos has united the human nature to itself, so as at the same time wholly to inhabit it and wholly to be outside it as being transcendent and infinite."[16]

This is why it simply will not do to say either *finitum non capax infiniti* or *infinitum capax finiti.* For classical Reformed theology, both are true, and we need to search for ways of saying both with equal seriousness: the infinite truly manifests itself in the finite, but the finite does not limit, encompass, exhaust, or enclose the infinite. The finite is circumscribed, borne, and contained by the infinite and it therefore cannot be separated from the infinite. Nevertheless, the infinite and the finite are never simply identical. The infinite participates in the finite, and so in a dependent sense the finite may be said to participate in the infinite, but there is always infinitely more than the finite comprehends. Statements such as these do not articulate foreign philosophical principles that govern Reformed Christology from without. They aim to express the full *intra-extra* dialectic that lies near the heart of Reformed eucharistic and incarnational theology.

THESES ON ECUMENICAL THEOLOGY

Reformed theology did not invent the *intra-extra* dialectic. Thus, Barth observed that Calvinists reverted to an earlier tradition in order to meet the innovation introduced by Luther and the Lutherans.[17] E. David Willis argues that Calvin's Christology is truly catholic in the sense that it continued a line of thinking found in theologians as diverse as Peter Lombard, Thomas Aquinas, Augustine, Origen, Theodore of Mopsuestia, Athanasius, and Cyril.[18] My chief concern here, however, is with the present. I want to suggest that the *intra-extra* dialectic may inspire dynamic contributions to contemporary theologies that cross boundaries and reach out to the *oikoumene.* I want to push the *intra-extra* dialectic—sometimes in ways that Calvin, Turretin, and the rest did not—in order to address a world they never knew.

The most important points may be summarized in six theses.

1. *Ecumenical theologies affirm that Jesus Christ is paradigmatic, without centering everything on Jesus.*[19]

The *intra-extra* dialectic encourages us to affirm that the infinite God is truly manifest in Jesus Christ without compromising Jesus' genuine and finite humanity. It therefore underscores the decisiveness of Jesus Christ, his particular life, ministry, death, and resurrection, for our apprehensions of the reality of God and of human life in appropriate relation to God. Jesus Christ is paradigmatic for our knowledge of God and of ourselves. But this is not the same thing as centering everything on Jesus. The *intra-extra* dialectic also encourages us to affirm that the Logos who is truly manifest in Jesus Christ is the same immeasurable reality who is universally present and active beyond the man Jesus as well.

These affirmations have important implications for where we may look in order to understand God and God's purposes. Thus, Calvin's doctrine of the knowledge of God is exclusively christological only in the sense that knowledge of God is available through Christ alone, who as the eternal Son, Logos, or Word cannot be restricted to the flesh or to the man Jesus. The Word, including its power to reveal God and God's purposes, is therefore also active among patriarchs and prophets. Indeed, the reach of the Word's revealing activity is coterminous with Christ's universal reign in nature and history beyond the man Jesus and also beyond the church. Thus, when Calvin noted certain universal standards of natural equity and civic fair dealing, he did not regard this "testimony of natural law and of that conscience which God has engraved on the minds of men" as something opposed to Christ. Justice embedded in the creative and providential ordering of nature is also the law of the eternal Son by whom and for whom all things were made.[20] In short, the *intra-extra* dialectic both complicates and broadens the question of appropriate sources of insight for theology and theological ethics.

Particularly among American Protestants, however, the faith of Christians sometimes is presented as if one's personal relationship with Jesus were the only important thing; as if the Christian scriptures contained only the New Testament; as if the Hebrew Scriptures were relevant only insofar as they pointed to the man from Nazareth; as if Jesus alone were humanity's only hope. Affirmations such as these reflect an exclusionary bias that encourages us to define Christianity as "true" and other religions as "false," to exaggerate the difference between Christian and Jewish faith, and to define the neighbor as our fellow Christian. They obscure Jesus' devotion to the one God who renders all persons and things an inclusive commonwealth or universe. In effect, they portray Jesus Christ as the Christian God, a unique, entirely known, and understood possession of the Christian community.[21]

The *intra-extra* dialectic inspires us to put forward ecumenical theologies that affirm Jesus Christ as paradigmatic disclosure of God and of human life in appropriate and responsive relation to God. It encourages us to attend to the specific revelatory pattern of what Jesus says, does, and endures that we find in the New Testament. However, it also encourages us to reject "Jesus-centrism," or the tendency simply to equate the infinite God with the man Jesus. Jesus-centrism displaces broader, trinitarian understandings of God. It inappropriately narrows the question of sources of insight for our knowledge of God, and it also dispels our sense of God's immensity, hiddenness, and incomprehensibility. Jesus-centrism denies the *extra* dimension essential to more capacious Christologies. Theologically understood, this is the source of its unfortunate exclusionary bias as well as of its truncated and self-recommending assumption that there is really nothing more to God than is manifest in Jesus and understood by the historic Christian community.[22]

2. *Ecumenical theologies emphasize that God the redeemer is the creator and that God the creator is the redeemer.*

The *intra-extra* dialectic emphasizes the affirmation that the eternal Word became flesh.[23] The Word who was in the beginning and was God, the Word through whom and for whom all things were made, has been made manifest in Jesus Christ the redeemer. Thus, Jesus Christ our sure redeemer manifests the creator who bears all things and in whom all things come to be. Or, to put this another way, the redeemer is the creator and the creator is the redeemer.

This affirmation supports a fundamental insistence that the world is neither opposed to redemption nor spiritually inert. In Christ, the entire universe (the inhabited world and more) is never "merely" material, "merely" historical, or "merely" natural. In Christ, the world is good creation, the active and present reign of the good God who redeems. It is the commonwealth of all things under God and on its way to promised redemption.

This is why capacious theologies informed by the *intra-extra* dialectic stand against merely interior and privatistic spiritualities that search for God by escaping the world. They understand new life in Christ as a faithful engagement in God's world. They regard the physical body, family, children, technology, commerce, government, and much more as parts of God's good creation in which we are encouraged to participate. Genuinely ecumenical theologies express a "worldly" piety that responds to the redeeming presence in Jesus Christ of the God who creates and upholds the world.

Particularly in an age of interdependent economies, burgeoning technologies, and advancing sciences, we should also note another corollary. The world of light and darkness, seas and land, vegetation, stars, planets, fish, birds, reptiles, cattle, delicate ecologies, destructive forces, and all that remains unknown is not just a prologue to redemption. It is more than an outsized stage for the dramas of human history. It is good creation, borne by the immeasurable heights and depths of God's creative and redemptive reign. It is the divinely ordered environment on which we depend and in which we participate, and it appropriately calls forth religious sensibilities of awe and wonder and respect.[24]

3. *Ecumenical theologies recognize that the world and all that is in it may become symbolic of the divine.*

The *intra* indicates that God and God's purposes are mediated in and through finite mundane realities. Were this not the case, theology would reduce to the entirely negative enterprise of surmising that, beyond the finite realities of nature and history, there may be an infinite mystery of which we know nothing at all. In fact, it is precisely the specific and particular patterns, textures, directions, shapes, and morphologies of finite and mundane media that help us to frame positive statements about God. *Infinitum capax finiti.* Therefore, the fertility of creatures may indicate that the creator is a God of life. The Exodus may suggest that God liberates the oppressed. Prophets may remind us that our responsibilities in society point toward a God of justice, and Jesus' practice of eating with tax collectors and sinners may portray God's unmerited grace and care.

Nevertheless, the *extra* dimension means that God cannot simply be identified with finite realities and the insights they suggest. Finite media do not encompass the divine; they do not allow us to manipulate or control it. Instead, they point beyond themselves toward the divine reality that transcends finite media. They point beyond themselves and so put us in touch with that which remains beyond our comprehension. *Finitum non capax infiniti.* Therefore, while God is manifest in the Exodus, the Exodus is not God. Although God liberates the oppressed, it does not follow that liberation is God. Even in the instance of God's preeminent manifestation, we do not simply equate God with the man Jesus. The reality of God is present in the man Jesus, but it does not follow that humanity is God. The Christ event authorizes the statement that God is love, but it does not follow that love is God. The *extra* dimension means that the relation to God is uninvertible. Statements about God that are made possible by the *intra* are rendered irreversible by the *extra*—by the recognition that the infinite God always and immeasurably transcends all finite realities.[25]

Here we come across a sacramental sensibility too often at risk in secular societies where life is reduced to rational-instrumental surfaces without depths: finite and mundane realities may become symbols of the divine.[26] They may suggest the capability of the infinite that constitutes the true depth of the finite. They may point to the divine touching the mundane. They may evoke the encompassing divine presence in which we live and move. *Infinitum capax finiti.* Therefore, like the bread and the wine, all other finite realities (including persons, historical occurrences, and the order of nature) may become signs that participate in the divine reality to which they point. In their specific textures and patterns, they may disclose God and make for communion. And yet, *finitum non capax infiniti.* Like the bread and wine, finite realities that are symbolic of the infinite remain what they are. They remain ordinary even as they communicate the extraordinary that is always the true depth of everything ordinary.[27]

We should also note that finite realities may become demonic "antisigns." In general, if the disenchantingly bland and secular tends to deny the *intra,* the demonic destroys the *intra-extra* dialectic by denying the *extra.* The problem here is therefore the opposite of the one presented by secular reductions of mundane realities to instrumental surfaces, although it may be that secular denials of the *intra* invite demonic distortions. The demonic distorts both the finite and the infinite by *identifying* a particular finite reality (itself) with the infinite itself. The demonic is a living idol, the finite laying claim to divine greatness for itself and thus suppressing its own ambiguity and ordinariness. As such, it wrecks the sacramental and the symbolic. It suggests the reality of the true God only and often terrifyingly by means of a kind of inversion, by pointing only to itself and refusing to point beyond itself. That is, it suggests the reality of the true God in the same way that every denial must also suggest and bring to mind that which it denies.[28]

4. *Ecumenical theologies recognize that our talk about God is symbolic, and they make use of many symbols.*

The task of ecumenical theology is to interpret the signs, to use language in order to say what ordinary, everyday, and worldly realities convey about God. The vitality of our talk about God therefore depends on its ability to evoke both the *intra* and the *extra. Infinitum capax finiti.* Talk about God evokes the *intra* when it points toward the mysterious presence of God that constitutes the true depth of mundane objects and occurrences. *Finitum non capax infiniti.* Talk about God evokes the *extra* when it points toward the mysterious Other whom we never entirely know or comprehend. In short, vital talk about God is evocative, and evocative talk about God is symbolic. It is a kind of poetry. Like a work of art, it enables us "to apprehend the familiar freshly and with new vision."[29]

To put this same point another way, symbolic talk about God refers to both God and world at the same time.[30] It furnishes patterns or schema of interpretation that encourage us to ask about mundane realities, the reality of God, and the adequacy of the proposed patterns or schema for bringing out the relationship between them. Or, again, symbolic talk about God functions as a hypothesis that encourages us to inquire about the mundane realities to which it points, about the all-encompassing divine reality, and about a proposed relation between them. This is how it precipitates interaction between knowers and the divine object that we know in and through other objects. This is how it facilitates conversation among people about how to understand and interpret the divine object that is mediated to us in and through our experiences of other objects.

For example, when we say that God is a liberator, we make a proposal about the relationship between divine reality and mundane occurrences such as the Exodus. We encourage both ourselves and others to ask whether and to what extent this relationship makes sense of other occurrences. We propose a discussion about interpreting God as liberator. We recall that our statements about God are irreversible and that it does not follow that liberation is God. Moreover, to the extent that this particular symbol seems inadequate to other objects in our experiences, we encourage conversations about how to understand God in other ways as well. For example, we also say that God is a judge, and so we make a proposal about the relationship between divine reality and mundane occurrences such as the Exile.

Talk about God loses its vitality when symbol and reality merge so that we no longer ask whether and how our symbol is adequate to that which remains beyond all comprehension. Then our language ceases to evoke wonder. Then it ceases to point beyond itself, and it ceases to be symbolic and poetic. Then we understand our words as vessels that contain and convey all that needs to be known rather than as instruments for exploration and discovery. And, as our words, their adequacy, and their function no longer are in question, we use our language to assert and proclaim in a manner that permits no further questions and no additional symbols. We reduce our words to technical terms that signify things completely known.

In sum, the *intra* means that our language can point to the encompassing reality of God. It means that we may speak rightly and evocatively of God in a manner that communicates knowledge. The *extra* supports a critical point made by some feminist theologians who object to the use of exclusively male imagery for God. As Johanna van Wijk-Bos puts it, "in considering how we may speak rightly of God, the discussion can never be closed. . . . God exceeds our designations, even our wildest imaginings."[31] This is why capacious and ecumenical theologies that are informed by the *intra* and the *extra* favor reflective poetry more than literal dogma. This is why they make use of many symbols and why they continue to raise questions about all symbols.

5. *Ecumenical theologies recognize that particular Christian subtraditions are indispensable but also open to continuing conversations and revisions.*

The plurality of Christian churches and theologies, the modern ecumenical movement, and the fact that so many Christians today know relatively little about the heritages of the churches to which they belong combine to raise the question of Christian subtraditions. If in Christ there is no east or west, does it really make sense that there are Roman Catholics, Russian Orthodox, Lutherans, Baptists, Presbyterians, Methodists, and so on? Do subtraditions have a legitimate place, or are they little more than disingenuous barriers to be overcome?

The *intra* means that the eternal Word does indeed come to us in and through particular finite media. Paradigmatically, God's Word comes to us in and through the particular man, Jesus of Nazareth. Therefore, this Word in Jesus Christ, this Gospel, is never available to us apart from the particulars of history. Indeed, the Word that comes to us in and through the historical particulars of Israel and Jesus Christ always invites historically particular symbolizations and interpretations by specific communities and subtraditions. On the other hand, the *extra* means that the Word of God who comes to us in and through particular finite media, and paradigmatically in Jesus, remains the inexhaustible and eternal Word who reigns in every place. Therefore, no particular symbolization, no specific tradition of interpretation, ever exhausts, captures, or entirely comprehends the Word of God in Jesus Christ.[32]

The Bible suggests this. We have in the New Testament four Gospels, renderings, or depictions of the Word manifest in Jesus Christ—five if you count Paul's letters as another. There are significant commonalities, and we recognize that they depict one Lord and one Word. Even so, the several renderings are not exactly alike in their literary styles, images, and depictions. They represent historically distinctive communities and/or subtraditions of symbolization and interpretation. None may be simply identified with *the Gospel* in a manner that displaces the others, and our Bibles would be impoverished were three or four eliminated in favor of presenting the remaining one as the single comprehensive depiction.

Instead, we acknowledge that the gospels point toward and witness to *the Gospel.* We affirm that we have no access to *the Gospel* or *the Word* apart from these particular interpretive witnesses. And yet, even when it comes to the literatures of the New Testament we insist that no one witness, no single interpretive community or tradition simply encompasses or possesses *the Gospel.* The solution? Put them side by side. Place them in conversation with one another and put Christians in conversation with all of them so that a fuller, more complete witness may emerge.

Similarly, the *intra-extra* dialectic encourages us to recognize that knowledge of God always comes to us in and through historical particulars, and that specific interpretive subtraditions remain indispensable. But it also reminds us that there is more to *the Gospel* than is dreamt of in our particular theologies and traditions. No tradition, no particular interpretation, encompasses or comprehends the Word of God. All remain partial and incomplete.

The solution? Put the subtraditions into conversation with one another. Keep them questioning the adequacy of their own symbols and interpretations in the light of the symbols and interpretations offered by others. On this view, ecumenical theologies do not supersede or displace particular Christian subtraditions; neither do they endorse dogmatic isolation. Ecumenical theologies emerge from particular subtraditions, they encourage conversations across subtraditions, and they endorse revisions that promise to support fuller and more faithful witnesses.

Ecumenically considered, then, the best Roman Catholic theology engages its particular heritage and subtradition of interpretation. It brings this subtradition into conversation with others, and it also remains open to the possibility that these conversations may lead to faithful and helpful emendations and revisions. The best

Reformed theology engages its own particular subtradition, its confessions, practices, theological treatises, and so on. It brings the Reformed subtradition into conversation with other, equally particular and partial Christian subtraditions, and it remains open to the possibility that these conversations may lead to vital and faithful revisions of Reformed theology.[33]

6. *Ecumenical theologies appreciate the importance of particular faith traditions as well as of continuing conversations among them.*

An explosion of information about religions of the world, travel to non-Christian countries, and massive migration from East to West have rendered the question of interreligious dialogue virtually unavoidable.[34] When we turn to this question, we sometimes come across universalistic attempts to construct a world theology. Here, insights drawn from Islam, Buddhism, Hinduism, Judaism, Christianity, and so on are taken to contribute to a global or human theology that is not Islamic, Buddhist, Hindu, Jewish, or Christian.[35] We also encounter exclusionary Christian theologies that define Christianity as "true" and other religions as "false." Other faiths are then taken into account by means of defensive apologetics and polemics aimed at demonstrating the superiority of Christian believing.[36]

Ecumenical Christian theologies informed by the *intra-extra* dialectic should be distinguished from both of these alternatives. As we have seen, the *intra* indicates that the reality of God is paradigmatically manifest in the life, ministry, death, and resurrection of Jesus Christ. It means that knowledge of God and God's purposes is mediated to us in and through finite mundane realities whose specific patterns, shapes, and textures enable us to make symbolic statements about God. It means that particular manifestations of God invite historically particular symbolizations and interpretations on the parts of specific communities, traditions, and subtraditions. The *extra* means that there are hidden depths of the immeasurable and encompassing reality of God. It means that God is universally present and active beyond the man Jesus as well as beyond the church, and it means that the communicative activity of God-in-Christ is finally coterminous with God's universal reign.

Informed by the *intra,* ecumenical theologies suspect that efforts to construct a world theology fail to estimate with sufficient seriousness the importance for our knowledge of God of particular media and traditions of interpretation. They suspect further that world theologies almost inevitably entail attempts to formulate common or generic concepts. And they note that such attempts may foreclose continuing conversations about the meaning and adequacy of the many symbols, reflective poetries, and interpretive heritages borne by the multitude of particular subtraditions and traditions.[37]

At the same time, an ecumenical theology informed by the *extra* rejects exclusionary theologies that do not recognize the limitations of their own symbols, traditions, and subtraditions, and that do not allow for the possibility of valid knowledge of God and God's purposes beyond the bounds of Christianity. It also suspects that defensive apologetics and polemics aimed at showing non-Christians why they should be Christians do relatively little to promote genuine interchange. Very often, they serve to insulate Christian communities from important questions that may arise in interfaith conversations.

Ecumenical theologies favor putting religious traditions and subtraditions into conversation with one another. They hope that these conversations will encourage us to appreciate distinctive features of our own traditions as well as commonalities among different traditions.[38] They hope that these conversations will keep us questioning the adequacy of our own symbols and interpretations in the light of insights offered by others. Here, the aim is neither a common world theology nor an impregnable defense of Christianity, but rather genuine conversations with worthy partners in our quests to know God more truly.[39]

ECUMENICAL AND REFORMED

Providentially and rightly, our contemporary situation calls for theologies that reach out toward the *oikoumene,* and in this essay I have tried to show that the Reformed Christian subtradition harbors significant christological resources for theologies that will do just that. I must now admit, however, that traditional Reformed theologians sometimes pressed these resources into the service of authoritarian and absolutistic outlooks that were closed to genuine interchange with other Christian subtraditions, let alone with other religions. Still, I think we have good reason to ask whether, when they did so, our forebears truly respected the *intra-extra* dialectic and what it communicates about God and about ourselves as finite knowers. Did they truly appreciate the dialectical and self-critical potential of their own theology of incarnation? Did they see its significance for the way we understand theological language? Did they suspect that it placed at the center of Christian theology a disclosive paradigm that can never be entirely grasped or exhausted, one that therefore pushes us to remain open to truth and insight wherever (in God's world) they may be found? In our present interdependent and pluralistic world, we may at least wonder whether we have good christological reasons to relinquish and revise authoritarian dimensions of traditional Reformed theology. We may wonder whether we have good christological reasons to broaden and extend the conversation begun at the Lord's Table.

Ecumenical theology is capacious, generous, and open rather than narrow, stingy, and closed. Indeed, only such a theology will adequately address our current circumstance. Nevertheless, the dynamic spirit of the Reformed Christian subtradition is worth explicating, promoting, deepening, and extending. I really do believe that we can and must have it both ways. Thus, my six theses are perhaps best understood as suggestions for ecumenical theologians who are also self-consciously (although neither slavishly nor uncritically) Reformed. This, too, I think, accords with the *intra-extra* dialectic: the way toward capacious theologies that cross barriers and boundaries lies in and through our particular communities, traditions, and subtraditions rather than outside of them or beyond them. This may be among the more important lessons to learn as we endeavor to engage our present world. Certainly, it is why even a musty old Calvinist idea about incarnation may yet have a truly contemporary and ecumenical relevance.

Part 2

A Community of Hopeful Realism

6 Engaging Culture

The gospel is the truth. As the apostle Paul writes, it "is the power of God for salvation," and in it are revealed the grace and righteousness and faithfulness and love of God (Rom. 1:16–17). This is why you and I are encouraged, inspired, and compelled to talk about it. This is why we are commissioned to talk about it.

AN INEXHAUSTIBLE DEPTH OF RICHES

Nevertheless, talking about the gospel, understanding it and expressing it, presents a perennial challenge. With Paul, you and I may affirm that "in Christ God was reconciling the world to Godself" (2 Cor. 5:19). Talking about the gospel is as simple as saying just this. And yet, like all simple statements of gospel truth, this one suggests that, in its simplicity and in its poetic fullness, the gospel remains an inexhaustible, mysterious, and even incomprehensible depth of riches. No matter what we say about it, there is always more to be said. The gospel is something to talk about, but it is always more than we can say.

This is one reason why, when we talk about the gospel, we speak knowing that in our speaking we never encompass or capture the gospel. We read Scripture, deliver sermons, say prayers, sing hymns, perform liturgies, and write confessions knowing all the while that we never translate the gospel without remainder. We never package it or possess it. We only—but we hope also faithfully—point toward the gospel and interpret it. We only—but we hope also faithfully—witness to the gospel.

Important consequences follow. Just because we recognize that there is always more to say, and just because we recognize that we cannot simply equate our witnesses with the gospel itself, we also recognize that there are ways of talking about the gospel other than our own ways. We do not therefore say that the gospel may be spoken and spoken of in literally any way at all. The gospel is the Word of God in Jesus Christ and, as such, has particular content. God was not doing just anything in Jesus Christ; "in Christ God was reconciling the world to Godself." And, in a world of fragmentation and conflict, not all words are reconciling. Not all words witness to the Word. Not all words witness to and further the work of restoring true communion with God in community with others. Not all words point toward the gospel. This should be enough to discredit the more blatant attempts to enlist the gospel in support of racial, religious, and national hatreds. Nonetheless, we do say that the Word of God in Jesus Christ, the particular content of the gospel, is such that there are always many ways to say what needs to be said. There are always many ways of witnessing to and participating in the work of reconciling people to God and to one another.

This is why, when it goes about the business of witnessing to the gospel, the church here and now does well to do much as it has always done in every age and in every place. It does well to witness to the gospel, to ponder the particular content of God's Word. At the same time, it also does well to multiply symbols, to say many things about the gospel, and to generate many perspectives on the gospel. It does well to develop faithful reflections that eschew detached descriptions of things completely known, and instead traffic in images, patterns, models, and paradigms that interpret but never entirely capture. For when the church properly estimates this inexhaustible depth of riches, it recognizes that there are more ways of talking about and witnessing to the gospel than are dreamt of in our theologies.

Moreover, when we turn our theology of sin back on ourselves, it quickly becomes apparent that our interpretations of the gospel always are interested and partial, and that our partial depictions of the gospel inevitably are skewed. This is something that Christians and their churches learn and relearn in almost every age. Thus, a church with an imperial history finds that it has emphasized hierarchy and neglected egalitarian dimensions of Jesus' life and ministry. A liberal movement imbued with the idea of human progress finds that it has neglected the action of God in history as well as eschatological themes. More recently, important distortions of the gospel and of the good and abundant life of communion with God in community with others have been exposed by liberationist and feminist theologians. But the general point is simply this. Not only is there always more to the gospel than we can say, but what we do say is always partial and hampered by some degree of distortion.

For much classical theology, this is a place where the doctrine of the Spirit and inspiration come in. The Spirit not only inspired the writers of scripture, it also continues to inspire readers, hearers, and interpreters. The Spirit is the source of truth wherever it may be found and, indeed, in this and other senses, John Calvin maintained that "all truth is of God."[1] This is also why so many liturgies contain a prayer for illumination just before the scriptures are read and interpreted. We recognize it to be beyond our powers of understanding to get the gospel just right. We recognize that we neither control nor entirely comprehend the Word of God and its meaning for us.

These are important concepts for Christians and their churches to grasp as they try to articulate and embody the truth of the gospel in any age, and most especially in a contentious one such as our own. Theology matters. And yet, when we honestly recognize the unavoidable need for humility and self-criticism, we faithfully refuse to equate our particular witnesses with the gospel itself. Then we recognize that there is always more to be said and that what we say is never free from distortion. Then we recognize that there are always ways of talking about the gospel other than our own. Then (and only then) the church is free to try its hand at renewing our encounter with an evangelical treasure that is ever ancient and ever new.

OUR CURRENT CIRCUMSTANCE

This brings us to a second critical point. Christians and their communities do not talk about the gospel in general or in the abstract. They talk about it in particular contexts. They witness to and participate in God's great reconciling work in Egyptian villages, or at Constantine's Rome, in Nazi Germany, in contemporary El Salvador, or in downtown Richmond, Virginia. They confront the gospel under the pressures of a current circumstance. Theologically considered, we should say that they witness to the gospel in response to what God is doing at a particular place and time.

Here, too, we should observe important notes of caution. The infinite God and great Author of history has done many things, is doing many things, and shall do many things in many communities, on many continents, and in many galaxies. As finite minds, we are unable to attend to everything at once, and so we attend selectively to limited contexts and configurations. We therefore never comprehend all that God is doing. Indeed, we never truly grasp the complete and final context for what we do apprehend of what God is doing. Theologically considered, then, our understanding of what God is doing in our current context (or in any other) always remains fragmentary and incomplete.

Moreover, like our understandings of the gospel, our interpretations of what God is doing are not only fragmentary and incomplete but also interested, partial, and skewed. In the midst of our involvements with the encompassing world, not only do we inevitably select in order to understand, but our selections are persistently responsive to inordinately partial interests and purposes. Our interpretations and depictions of circumstances and contexts calling for action, therefore, chronically leave out of account interrelations, situations, and consequences that are important to others. One thinks, for example, of Puritan interpretations of their great migration to New England—they rarely seem to have asked what God was doing in a manner that was responsive to the interests of America's native inhabitants. In sum, not only are our understandings of what God is doing always fragmentary and incomplete, but our partial interpretations of what is going on always suffer some degree of distortion. This is why we need to put forward our own estimates of our current circumstances self-critically and with an appropriate tentativeness and humility.

This is yet another place where the doctrine of the Spirit and illumination enter in. Our visions and interpretations are influenced by conditions, circumstances, events, and passions that lie beyond our control. True interpretations of the signs of the times are therefore not easily obtained. Indeed, as both prophets and politicians often recognize, we cannot simply conjure one up whenever we please.

CHANGING CULTURAL LOCATION

Now, with all of these cautions in mind, let me nevertheless hazard the following. In our own place and time, one thing that is going on is this: the "mainline" churches are in transition. Their cultural location is changing. Sociologists and historians tell us that this is part of a broader realignment and restructuring of American religion.[2] As the nation has become more and more ethnically and religiously diverse, as Catholicism has emerged to champion elements of the historic liberal agenda, as conservative Protestantism has made an impressive bid to become a culture-shaping force, and as growing numbers of Americans find spiritual meaning in experiences, explorations, and ideas apart from established institutional forms, the religious and moral center has become increasingly fragmented.

The restructuring of American religion is itself a part of even wider cultural developments. It connects with the felt sense of some people and communities that American society is more flexible and more open to their distinctive contributions. It also connects with the felt sense of others that American society has lost its moral compass, as well as with worries about the place of the "Western canon" in our educational curricula. In any case, mainstream Protestantism no longer dominates. It no longer shapes the religiocultural agenda with a broadly compelling authority. A spate of recent books, articles, and denominational reports points toward "mainstream Protestant decline." Indeed, some sociologists and historians prefer to speak of "oldstream" or "oldline" Protestantism, a movement that now has been decisively displaced. We may agree at least that the "oldline" Protestant churches in America have recently experienced a significant devaluation of their cultural authority.

My initial point here is simply this. When those of us who are associated with these "mainline" or "oldline" churches witness to God's great reconciling work, when we talk about the gospel in America today, we do so under the pressure of this shift in our cultural circumstance.

I think that we can understand important aspects of this pressure with the help of an analogy. Where I grew up, the biggest kid on the block often found it comparatively easy to participate in nearly every game of stickball or hoops. He was the-force-to-be-reckoned-with. But it was tougher if you were smaller. Then, participation was no longer automatic. You really had to be committed to playing, and you had to devote time and energy to figuring out just how you were going to participate.

Somewhat similarly, the most influential religious communities and institutions often find it comparatively easy to participate in their wider world. They can do so almost without thinking. But the going gets tougher when you are less influential. Participation is no longer automatic. Now it requires explicit commitment, effort, deliberation, and attention. This is why the mainline or oldline churches in America today face some pressing challenges. Shall we continue to participate in our society and culture now that we no longer are the biggest and most influential kid on the block? Shall we retreat into the private and personal or into the churchy and ecclesiastical? Shall we look on our decentering, our shift in cultural location, as an opportunity to become more deliberate and intentional about the ways in which we participate in and engage our world? If I am correct, then in and through a somewhat traumatic shift in our cultural location, God is calling us to reflect seriously, explicitly, and creatively about the manner of our faithful participation in the world.

SOME GOSPEL TRUTHS

As we approach the good news of God's reconciling act in Jesus Christ under the pressures of this particular circumstance, we recognize that others must also approach it under other pressures in other circumstances in Latin America and in Russia and in Africa.

Nonetheless, we also recognize that the challenge that comes to the fore for us concerns our willingness and courage to pursue a course of faithful engagement and participation even during a period of cultural displacement. In the light of this challenge, I think we do well to recall four interrelated elements of the symbolic framework of Christian theology. The gospel tells the truth about God and world, sin and grace, motives and morality, and church and world.

God and World

The gospel tells the truth about God and world. The world belongs to God. This is something that we learn in the opening chapters of Genesis and throughout the biblical narrative. Here we run across a fundamental point that sets the context for all of the others. All things in nature and in history are caught up in an intricate web of divine power, presence, and purpose. Thus, the nineteenth-century liberal theologian Friedrich Schleiermacher claimed that all things are bound up in a single divine causality.[3] The Dutch prime minister and theologian Abraham Kuyper emphasized "*the sovereignty of the Triune God over the whole cosmos,* in all of its spheres and kingdoms, visible and invisible."[4] We might say that the reign of God is what renders the many a *uni*verse. No area of life, no corner of creation, lies beyond the activity of God. And, in the light of the challenge facing us today, we may observe that this is why we are called to respond faithfully to God in all areas of life. Human life is response or reply to the prior divine activity, and the divine activity meets us everywhere.[5]

There is still more to be said. In Jesus Christ, the God to whom we respond in all areas of life, the God who creates and governs the world, is also the One who reconciles the world. The God who creates and sustains is the redeeming Word; the Word, or the principle of redemption, is the God who creates and sustains (John 1). The great God of glory who creates and bears all things in nature and in history is the good God of grace who redeems.

This radical statement about the God to whom the world belongs also tells us something more about the world. The world not only belongs to God and is not only a universe. The world is also the present reign of God the creator, sustainer, and redeemer. Rather than some whirring cosmic accident, it is a reality with a trajectory and direction. The world is God's good creation and reign ordered toward reconciliation and redemption. God values contingent existence; God values the world.

Therefore, our faithful response or reply to God's activity does not mean withdrawal or escape from the world so much as a new quality of responsiveness to and involvement in the world. In the light of the gospel, the cosmos of planets and people and schools and stars and music and rocks and urban squalor and weather and agriculture and frogs and armies and businesses and bushes and more is the great drama of reconciliation, the theater of God's glory within which we live and move and respond to God and to others at every turn.

We deny the truth about God and world whenever we restrict the range of our faithful participation in God's world. In America today, we often do so in different, almost diametrically opposed ways. Captivated by otherworldly spiritualities, we may limit faithfulness to what is personal, private, and interior, and thereby neglect the physical, social, public, and institutional. Again, our commitments to social action sometimes leave out the personal and the interior as well as our interrelations with nature. Spiritualities concerned for the integrity of nature sometimes lead us to neglect political and economic dimensions of social justice.

To these and to all other restrictive pieties a contemporary witness to the gospel will suggest a more capacious and holistic spirit. It will reply that nothing exists apart from God. It will insist that we are called to respond faithfully to God in every area of life. In word and in deed, it will proclaim that, in Jesus Christ, God was reconciling the world—and certainly nothing less than all the world—to Godself.

Sin and Grace

The gospel of reconciliation indicates that God values the world and that we are called to participate faithfully in God's world. It envisions the world as God's reign. But, of course, if in Christ God reconciles the world, then the world must also stand in need of reconciliation. If Jesus Christ is redeemer, then there also must be something from which the world needs to be redeemed. And this brings us to a second point. The gospel tells the truth about sin and grace.

You know the story. Having made humankind on the sixth day, "God saw everything that he had made, and indeed, it was very good" (Gen. 1:31). We humans are parts of a good creation. We are fitted for an abundant and good life together in God's encompassing reign, a life in which we deploy our powers and capacities in responsible interrelations with God and others. We are created in the image of God. And yet, it is also true that "there is no one who is righteous. . . . All have turned aside. . . . All have sinned and fall short of the glory of God" (Rom. 3:10, 23; Ps. 14:1–3, 53:1–3). Communion with God and community with neighbor are broken. We are adrift in a history of fragmentation, conflict, massive suffering, and violence. And as judge, God gives us over to the consequences of our sin.

Thus, John Calvin thought that human beings are mirrors of God's wisdom, goodness, and power. He claimed that we are endowed with wondrous capacities, and that God's image originally shone in their upright arrangement.[6] However, he also believed that sin means radical and universal derangement. Sin infects all of our capacities as well as every aspect and institution of society (including the church), and it continues to produce a train of evil consequences. Somewhat similarly, the American Puritan Jonathan Edwards noted that sin is an active and persistent tendency, an orienting impulsion, and a disposing misalignment of our powers.[7] We might say that we are not now what we are fitted to be. The human fault is both radical and universal, and so the human project is unavoidably skewed.

Nevertheless, grace abounds. God is judge, but not only judge. The faithful God also refuses to abandon wayward creatures. The faithful God keeps faith with faithless sinners. For one thing, as Calvin, Edwards, and others noted, God continues to uphold in fallen persons impressive abilities in the arts and sciences, as well as certain basic social affections and a rudimentary sense of justice or fairness.[8] By means of providential care and of judgment, the law, covenants, and prophets, God restrains human corruption, God calls us back, and God guides us toward good. Moreover, in Jesus Christ, God regenerates. Sin's dominion is broken, and human powers and capacities begin to be realigned.

Regenerating grace brings renewed possibilities. Thus, Calvin claimed that our capacity for well-doing is restored by grace and the Spirit, and that the basic fruits are piety toward God and charity toward neighbor.[9] Edwards thought that grace supports true virtue or a disposition of benevolence to being-in-general. The nineteenth-century American Horace Bushnell claimed that persons are brought to a new reigning love, so that "life proceeds from a new center."[10] Another way to express this good news is to say that, by God's reconciling grace, the possibility and destiny from which we have been alienated and separated are restored. The possibility and destiny of true communion with God in community with others are restored. Jesus Christ, the power of God for salvation, introduces a new vitality and "newness of life" (Rom. 6:4).

We deny the truth about sin and grace, corruption and kingdom, whenever we overlook the bad and minimize the good. We deny it when we fail to apprehend the seriousness of the human fault and the severity of divine judgment. We deny it when we underestimate God's faithfulness and so fail to look for grace and new possibilities.

Among more than a few Protestants today, such denials have taken root in worship itself. Consider services without either prayers of confession or assurances of pardon; where we lament no fault, we anticipate no remedy. Upbeat services of worship from which all mention of sin has been expurgated may appeal to American seekers, but they truncate the gospel. They seem popular partly because they bolster faltering self-esteem, but they also endorse a wishful and tragically naive optimism that underestimates the destructive bent of persons, communities, and institutions. Trusting that everyone is O.K. (especially ourselves), we fail to pursue realistic strategies and structures of restraint. And then, when the good is not preserved, when corruption proves both fearsome and persistent, we tumble into cynicism and despair. Then, there emerges a thoroughgoing defensiveness, a timid pessimism so unamazed by grace and opportunities for renewal that it endorses only restraints and so fails to take risks that might make things better.

In the face of humdrum philosophies of life that celebrate heights without depths even as they embrace limits apart from possibilities, a contemporary witness to the gospel will claim that sin and grace, judgment and reconciliation belong together. It will insist that we ought not deceive ourselves and yet that we ought never give up hope. It will say that we ought to denounce and restrain corruption, but also that we ought to announce and pursue promising possibilities for genuine communion and renewal. It will push us to move beyond both naive optimism and defensive pessimism. It will encourage us to become hopeful realists.

Motives and Morality

God's great act of reconciliation encourages us to participate faithfully in God's world and supports a hopefully realistic outlook or vision that combines attitudes of pessimism and optimism. But it also furnishes moral guidance. In part, it does this by reordering both inward disposition and outward action in thankful response to the gifts and grace of God. Looked upon in the light of our current circumstance, the gospel tells the truth about motives and morality.

For one thing, it challenges our typically prudential reasons for being moral. Within the frame of the gospel, you and I should not be moral or just or good because we believe that we shall merit salvation or else gain some sort of cosmic credit by either our moral commitment or our performance. We won't. As Paul well understood, the good news of the gospel is a message of free reconciliation and forgiveness (Rom. 3:21–26, 5:12–21; Gal. 2:15–21). Jesus Christ discloses the faithful God-for-others who calls creatures into being and who sustains them and redeems them quite apart from their merits. In this context, morality is not a defensive attempt at self-recommendation, but a song of thankfulness, gratitude, and praise rooted in an apprehension of the most excellent faithfulness of God.

This does not mean that motive is the only thing, or that God's free faithfulness and grace simply put an end to moral standards. God's reconciling act in Jesus Christ has a particular shape and form. Jesus Christ teaches and embodies the true communion with God in community with others that characterizes the kingdom. He does not come to abolish the law or the prophets (Matt. 5:17). Indeed, law remains a form of the gospel. Thus, we are called to follow the way of the person-for-others who healed the sick and ate with outcasts. We are enjoined to love God and neighbor. We are commanded to love our enemies and to refrain from retaliating (Matt. 22:34–40 par.; 5:38–48). Again, we are admonished to live by the Spirit and to bear one another's burdens (Gal. 5:25). We are reminded that love does not rejoice at wrongdoing, and we are admonished to do justice and love kindness (1 Cor. 13:4–7).

In short, the gospel indicates that faithfulness is a matter of internal motives and dispositions but also of external standards, practices, and behavior. This is a critical point for Christian ethics and one that lay near the center of Karl Barth's controversy with "German Christians" who attempted to separate piety and politics. "What these good folk obviously want," Barth wrote, "—a Church that is only inward and not at all outward—is identical with what National Socialism wants of the Church."[11]

We forget the gospel truth about motives and morality whenever we subvert the pattern and direction of reconciliation. In America today, we sometimes do this by reducing life to the pursuit of competitive advantages and individual rewards.[12] Partly in response to some interpretations of a free market economy, we affirm and embody the opposite of true communion and community. Reversing Paul's admonition in Philippians 2:4, we picture all of life as an enterprise of looking out for "number one," and for our own isolated interests rather than the interests of others. Then again, we also forget the truth about motives and morality when we reduce the life of faith only to externals or only to internals. We deny it whenever we moralistically imagine that the sum total of faithfulness is right actions and practices, and so neglect the importance of heart, spirit, intention, and disposition. We also deny it whenever we insist that faithfulness and spirituality are entirely inward, and so neglect the importance of action, policy, practice, and institution.

In response to these pernicious reductions—these diminutions of faith and ethics—a contemporary witness to the gospel of reconciliation in Jesus Christ will testify that there are more fundamental, powerful, and appropriate sensibilities and motives at work in human life than one's own isolated interest and advantage. It will also insist that genuine faithfulness is a matter of the whole person, that external standards without internal dispositions are dead, and that dispositions without external standards are blind.

Church and World

God and world, sin and grace, motives and morality. But this is not all. The gospel also tells the truth about church and world.[13] It tells us that the church is a society or an association of common life and practice, rather than a lone believer or a mere collection of individuals. It tells us that the church is a new community gathered in the Spirit and overcoming division "where two or three are gathered together" (Acts 2; Matt. 18:20). It tells us that the church is also an institution, a body with many members who perform different functions (1 Cor. 12:12–31; Eph. 4:1–16).

This society, association, and institution always acknowledges, depends on, points toward, and recognizes something prior to and more fundamental than itself. The church is the company of those who acknowledge God's reconciling way with the world in Jesus Christ. It recognizes and appropriates the way of grace that goes over to betrayers in order to reconcile and to reestablish good and abundant life. It acknowledges that God creates the world, judges the world, sustains the world, and redeems the world. The church is the community and institution that understands it cannot say or think "God" without also saying and thinking "world." The church is the company of those who recognize that "to be reconciled to God is to be sent into the world as God's reconciling community."[14]

As such, the church always finds itself caught up in a dynamic interrelation with the world. "Go therefore and make disciples of all nations . . ." (Matt. 28:19). The church is *in* the world because, as a matter of mission, it is sent to everyone everywhere. This is why it intentionally mixes into the world and why it goes to every person in every location and condition. And, of course, when it really does go to everyone everywhere, the church demonstrates that the gospel crosses boundaries. Then, it demonstrates that the way, the truth, and the life is not shut in, localized, or confined. Then, it embodies the reconciling truth that, in Jesus Christ, no person or community is either alien or strange.

Lamentably, the willingness of both church and society to cross boundaries and to testify to a genuinely inclusive community under God has now become a pressing concern. Consider some recent occurrences. The Glorious Church of God in Christ at Richmond, Virginia, is burned. City leaders at Greenville, South Carolina, say that homosexuality is at odds with local community standards. Seminary faculty are criticized for inviting a noted feminist theologian to speak on their campus. The Presbyterian Church (U.S.A.)

refuses gay ordination. What shall we say? Surely that the church is a reconciling community that has been sent to everyone everywhere. Surely that we have been sent to build up a single community where there are no outsiders and no insiders, no first-class citizens and no second-class citizens. Surely that we are to welcome one another just as Jesus Christ has welcomed us, for the glory of God (Rom. 15:7).

The church is *with* the world confessing common faults and sins. Because it knows that "there is no one who is righteous, not even one"—not even itself (Rom. 3:10; Ps. 14:3, 53:3), the church attempts both to embody and to call for self-criticism and repentance. It attempts to criticize its own life and practice in the light of the gospel of true communion with God in community with others, and it tries to remain open to criticisms offered by others. At the same time, of course, this must also mean that the church is no easy friend of the world (James 4:4). Indeed, it may find itself *against* the world in prophetic denunciations and resistance, sometimes at significant cost to itself. Even when the world dismisses it as odd or insignificant, the church refuses to leave the world alone. It criticizes idols and corrupting constrictions. It focuses attention on injustice and the suffering of innocents.

Nevertheless, in all of these things, the church's passionate witnesses always press toward new possibilities. They envision a new heaven and a new earth (Rev. 21:1). Thus, in all of the many things that the church does, it is also and fundamentally true that the church is *for* the world. It is for a world reconciled and transformed. It is for human beings as well as for all creatures in their appropriate interrelations to God and to one another. The church announces that God is faithful, that grace abounds, and that therefore sin, fragmentation, and conflict are never the only or the last words. The church is for the reign of God. The church is a community of hope.

We deny the truth about church and world whenever we forget that these two are providentially imposed partners and that, theologically speaking, they cannot properly be understood apart from one another. Perhaps we try to be church without passionately, intentionally, and critically engaging the world. Perhaps we try to be world apart from church, apart from confronting the message and the ministry of reconciliation. But a community that does not go out from itself and has not yet engaged the world has not yet truly engaged God's reconciling Word and therefore can only be one that has not yet truly become church. And a world that has not yet confronted the message of sin and grace, judgment, reconciliation, and renewal has not yet begun to guess what it is intended to be.

THEOLOGY AND MISSION

The gospel is an inexhaustible depth of riches that is always more than we can say, and, indeed, our situated interpretations of it always remain fragmentary and distorted. But this does not mean that we are unable to witness to the gospel in our own time and place. It means rather that when we do so by grace and the Spirit, we should do so with an appropriate measure of self-criticism and humility. We should remember that there are always ways of talking about and witnessing to the gospel other than our own. We should remember that our own ways always remain subject to emendation and correction.

How shall those of us affiliated with "oldline" Protestant churches in America respond to the devaluation of our cultural clout and authority? If I am correct, when we interpret the gospel in the light of this question, we find that it tells us the truth about God and world, sin and grace, motives and morality, and church and world. Moreover, when once we begin to confront these truths, to understand them, internalize them, and embody them, I believe that we will not retreat into privatized religion, or into some other form of otherworldliness. Neither will we endorse recent calls to reject the world and to center everything on the community called church. Recognizing that the steadfast creating, judging, sustaining, and redeeming God is not absent from any part of the human project, recognizing that God is faithful, we will commit ourselves anew to the project of participating faithfully in God's world. We will be hopeful realists who denounce and restrain corruptions but also announce and pursue promising possibilities. We will be disciples who are beginning to be reordered in both our motives and our actions. We will sustain and nourish churches that are in, with, against, and for the world.

The providential gift of our cultural decentering should prod us to become more deliberate about our theologies and our engagements. In the midst of a dizzying plurality of outlooks and cosmopolitan institutions and roles that seem able to orient much of life quite apart from explicit religious sensibilities, we need to remember that theology matters. People will not be formed by the truths of the gospel simply by virtue of their participation in contemporary American society. This is why we need to take the time and expend the institutional effort to equip persons with an integral and dynamic Christian confession. At the same time, in the midst of globally linked economic and political realities, vulnerable natural ecologies, powerful technologies, persistent injustice, and massive suffering, we need to remember that mission matters. People will not faithfully witness to the truths of the gospel without persistently and passionately engaging God's world in all of its current complexity and ambiguity. This is why we need to take the time and expend the institutional energy to denounce and restrain corruption and to announce and pursue promising possibilities for genuine communion and renewal.

Elsewhere I have suggested that efforts such as these may require additional commitments to theological education in congregations, seminaries, institutes, "think tanks," colleges, and universities, as well as a resurgence in good-quality church-related journalism. Clearly, they also may require renewed and additional institutionalizations of outreach and witness both locally and globally. But, whatever the particulars, the really important point is this. The characteristic mark of these ventures will be that they *combine* dynamic theological reflection with mission. They will not only talk about the gospel, they will also witness to it. They will not only witness to the gospel, they will also talk and reflect about their attempts at faithful witness. They will furnish opportunities for conversation about God and ourselves in the context of an engaging ministry of reconciliation that aims to enhance true communion in community. And so, by fits and starts, fragmentarily and provisionally, they will both witness to and reflect on the truth of the gospel. "In Christ God was reconciling the world to Godself" (2 Cor. 5:19).

7 The Ministry of Reconciliation

"The ministry of reconciliation" has always seemed to me to be an almost magical phrase. When I hear it, I think of the apostle Paul and his fledgling contentious churches. I think of the social gospel. I think of Martin Luther King Jr. I think of a young associate minister delivering an antiwar sermon. And I think of them all at once. I picture a witness, a kind of leadership, and a way of going about things connected less with calculation and competitive advantage than with the great adventure of genuine community against long odds. I picture a mission and a passionate commitment that fragment and falter again and again, and so stand in need of renovation and renewal again and again.

UNDERSTANDING MINISTRY

The church's ministry is a complicated practice that may be studied from the perspectives of a variety of disciplines. Historians may investigate changing understandings of ministry and its functions at different places and times. Sociologists may comment on the different roles and institutional structures that have been devised to carry out ministry. Several recent writers make use of theories of management and administration in order to clarify different styles of ministerial leadership.[1]

Ministry may also be understood in different ways within the poetic framework of Christian theology, partly because different images and symbols encourage somewhat different angles of vision on the church's ministry. For example, the Puritan Richard Baxter made use of the images of shepherd and flock in order to emphasize the pastoral relation of a minister to a congregation. He put special attention on the care and formation of the people of God.[2] If we look on ministry as an apostolic activity, we focus on handing on a message and building up the Christian community. When we speak of prophetic ministry, we recall the shrill voices of Jeremiah, Amos, and others, and we underscore social criticism and action.

In 2 Corinthians 5:18, Paul says that God has given us "the ministry of reconciliation." Here, emphasis falls on a fundamental pattern behind and beneath many ministerial functions, roles, structures, and relations. Here, we come across an image that goes to the heart of the gospel as well as to the heart of what it means to be church.[3] How shall we understand it?

GOD'S RECONCILING ACTIVITY

Reconciliation is one of the great images of the gospel because it intimates the entire history of redemption.[4] It points to the reestablishment of a broken relationship against the dark background of a lost wholeness and estrangement.[5] Reconciliation means God's re-creation of the world that has turned away from God, God's realization of God's original aim or purpose.

Karl Barth maintained that reconciliation is God's resumption of a society, a covenantal community of mutual interrelation and responsibility that was threatened by dissolution and destruction.[6] Somewhat similarly, H. Richard Niebuhr claimed that the reconciliation of people to God as well as of people to one another and to their world is the cause of Jesus Christ. "The establishment of this friendship," Niebuhr wrote, is "the key problem in human existence."[7]

"In Christ God was reconciling the world to Godself" (2 Cor. 5:19). This simple and elegant statement of the gospel takes the form of a witness to God's reconciling activity. It points to God overcoming alienation and division. It points to God establishing and renewing the true communion with God in community with others for which we have been fitted and sustained all along. Despite our tragic and persistent turning away from God and one another, in Jesus Christ, God goes out from Godself in order to re-create and resume a jeopardized and broken society. This reconciling activity of God in Jesus Christ is both logically and historically prior to the church and its ministry. Theologically speaking, this activity, this establishment of new possibility, forms the context for Paul's statement that God "has given us the ministry of reconciliation."

Now, in this context, one thing we should say is that reconciliation is in the particular pattern of Jesus Christ and what he says, does, and endures. Reconciliation is Christomorphic. It takes the form of the faithful person-for-others who teaches love of God and neighbor, the Word of God who crosses boundaries and breaks down barriers, healing the sick, blessing the poor, eating with outcasts, tax collectors, and sinners. It takes the shape of the one who lived and died and rose again for the cause of bringing people to God and so also of reconciling them to one another and to their world. Reconciliation is a matter of overcoming separation and division between God and ourselves and between ourselves and others. God's reconciling activity is a matter of cross and resurrection, of new life and new community emerging from brokenness, suffering, and death.

A MINISTRY IN AND FOR THE WORLD

Another, related thing we should say is that the ministry of reconciliation is a ministry in and for the world. It is not narrow or shut in. It is outgoing and capacious. This we know because our commission to minister, God's reconciling activity in Jesus Christ, is itself in and for the world. In John 3:16, we read that "God so loved the world that he gave his only Son." Paul insists that in Christ, God was reconciling the world and nothing less than the world to Godself. And, commenting on 2 Corinthians 5:19, John Calvin notes that reconciliation in Christ has "its source in the overflowing love of God."[8] We might say that in Christ the God who creates, sustains, and redeems does not remain shut in or closed up. God does not keep to Godself, and God does not go into seclusion. In Christ, God goes out to the world, and so, in Christ, the church is sent to all nations (Matt. 28:19). The ministry of reconciliation is a ministry in and for the world.

Now, if God's reconciling activity is in and for the world, and if the ministry of reconciliation is in and for the world, then it also must be that the world stands in need of reconciliation. You know the story. Having made humankind on the sixth day, "God saw everything that he had made, and indeed, it was very good" (Gen. 1:31). We humans participate in a good creation. We are fitted for an abundant and good life together in God's encompassing reign, a life in which we may deploy our considerable powers and capacities in responsible interrelations with God and others. Nevertheless, it is also true that "there is no one who is righteous. . . . All have turned aside. . . . All have sinned and fall short of the glory of God" (Rom. 3:10, 23; Ps. 14:1–3, 53:1–3).

We chronically deploy our powers and capacities to divide and destroy. Our practical reasoning is curved in on ourselves and our own isolated interests. We love the wrong things, or else the right things wrongly. We fail to uphold our responsibilities to others. In addition, there is no person, community, or institution that is exempt from sin's effects. Sin is radical and universal. Therefore, we find ourselves adrift in a cycle of fragmentation, conflict, mass suffering, and violence in which true communion with God and community with neighbor are broken.[9]

Such a world stands in need of reconciliation because it stands in need of love of God and neighbor. It stands in need of new community overcoming division. It stands in need of true communion with God in community with others. It stands in need of loyalty to the universal commonwealth of all persons, animals, plants, and things in their appropriate interrelations with God and with one another. It stands in need of devotion to the kingdom of God.

And, of course, such a world is a hard and difficult place that stands in need of reconciliation precisely because it is not much open to reconciliation. Indeed, altogether too often, the world seems hell-bent on going straight the other way. Even the newspapers testify: economic exploitation and political oppression, genocidal wars, mass starvation, child abuse, car bombs, police assaults, racism, homophobia, the debilitating destruction of natural environments and ecologies, and more.

A QUESTION AND AN ANSWER

The world stands in need of reconciliation and is not much open to it. This is an important, sobering (and, one is tempted to say, empirically verifiable) fact. But there is another fact that often seems especially disheartening to Christians and their communities: the church itself stands in need of reconciliation. Frequently, it finds itself infiltrated by the world's many alienations and divisions. Occasionally, in bursts of perverse creativity, it devises distinctive alienations and divisions on its own. When it comes to fragmentation, conflict, and disruption, the church stands with the world rather than above, beyond, or apart from the world.[10]

Those of us affiliated with "oldline" churches in America today—denominations that seem constantly occupied with crises, controversies, and potential splits—ought perhaps to be especially aware of this. (If you are having trouble, ponder the past few General Assemblies of the Presbyterian Church (U.S.A.).) But when we step back and consider longer frames of reference, we see that it has always been so. (Surely, the Corinthian congregation to which Paul wrote was no model of harmony, and in this it appears to have anticipated the bulk of ecclesiastical history.[11]) The church is racked by fragmentation and conflict: Jew and Gentile, north and south, east and west, Greek Orthodox, Roman Catholic, Protestant, conservative and liberal, male and female, rich and poor, black, white, brown, and red, gay and straight, urban, suburban, and rural. It is enough to make us wonder (as we know others also have wondered) why we should have been sent in the first place.

In this way, Christians and their communities arrive at a fundamental question: *How shall we, who are fragmented, alienated, and divided, undertake a ministry of reconciliation in and for a fragmented, alienated, and divided world?* The question remains unanswered so long as we focus our attention and concern, first and foremost, on the church's own righteousness, on its own abilities and disabilities, virtues and vices. How shall we undertake a ministry of reconciliation? The answer is that, in the midst of our fragmentation and conflict, a strange thing has happened. The answer is that "in Christ God was reconciling the world to Godself." This prior activity is the condition for the possibility of the ministry of reconciliation.

Indeed, just here, in a poor Jew crucified on an obscure hill, we have come to believe that a new possibility has arisen. We have come to believe that, by his life, ministry, sacrifice, and resurrection, all have been called to repentance and new life. We have come to believe that this darkest folly demonstrates the power of God made perfect in weakness, the grace of God that empowers persons and communities to live not only for themselves but also for God and for others. We have come to believe that corruption, alienation, and violence are neither the only nor the last words. We have come to believe that God holds to God's original and saving purpose, and that God's reconciling reign draws near.

NEW SIGHT

This is the mystery of God's reconciling act in Jesus Christ, the mystery of the cross and the resurrection, and in its light we have been given new vision and new sight.[12] We have begun to envision things differently. We have begun to see both church and world in a different perspective and from a different point of view. We have begun to see traces of God's reconciling activity, and so we have begun to envision all things anew.

We have begun to see traces of reconciling grace in the church when we gather together for worship. For then, especially as we gather in the midst of our divisions, we testify to the promise of a new community overcoming divisions in the presence of God. Then, however fleetingly, both despite and because of our fragmentation and our conflicts, we become a living symbol of the possibility of true communion with God in community with others. Then, we point (however distantly and inadequately) toward the good and abundant life for which we have been fitted and sustained.

We have begun to experience the new possibility when we attend to the story of Jesus Christ, the Word who discloses the faithful God-for-others, the person-for-others who discloses what it is to be truly human. We have begun to grow and to be nourished in the renewed possibility when we participate together in the Lord's

Supper. Indeed, the Supper becomes a sacramental embodiment of the true communion in community that is the ultimate aim of God's reconciling activity as well as the saving substance of God's reign. And, as we invite people to it by saying that "they will come from east and west, and from north and south to sit at table in the kingdom of God," the Supper becomes both a sacramental embodiment and an eschatological anticipation that is subversive of present orders that aid and abet fragmenting divisions.[13]

This is not all. We have also begun to glimpse traces of God's reconciling activity in the world. Perhaps we encounter a teacher who, when faced with limited resources as well as constant public uncertainty and debate about the aims of education, nevertheless strives to keep in view the needs, feelings, experiences, and interests of his or her students. Perhaps we remember an organization that, at significant cost to its leadership and its members, pursued a course of nonviolent resistance and confrontation in order to advance the participation of an oppressed minority and also to witness to the possibility of a more blessed and just political community for all. Perhaps we become acquainted with the routinely moving fidelity of a husband who cares for his wife through years of trying illness. Perhaps we know a city where churches refuse to allow elected officials to keep them from feeding the homeless. A country long ravaged by the grip of apartheid takes a fundamental turn.

There is more. Through cruciform spectacles, we also envision traces of God's reconciling activity even in the midst of brokenness. Now the exploitations and oppressions, the genocides, starvations, and ecological disasters, the abuses, hatreds, and injustices no longer appear as determinative testimonies to the corrupted way things are and must always be. Now we see them as judgments. Now we believe that, in and through these many Calvaries, God calls us to repentance and new possibility. (Turned from hatred by the continuing holocaust of violence, suffering, and fear, courageous people in Northern Ireland take up the cause of peace and try to make room for a political solution. I am also reminded of the following incident. Some months ago, a Jordanian soldier shot some Israeli schoolgirls before his fellow soldiers were able to stop him. King Hussein, and his son and daughter (two children who surely live under constant threat), visited the homes of the killed and wounded children.

There they knelt, prayed, and asked forgiveness. It was a liturgic act of leadership on the part of the Muslim monarch, as well as a much needed trace of God's reconciling activity in a shattered world.)

Whether it is that vision falters or that the restorative effects of judgment too often fail to materialize, we obviously do not see such things always and everywhere. Much of what takes place in our churches seems merely humdrum, compromising, and disappointing. Much of what takes place in the wider world seems only to threaten and destroy. For myself, I admit that, altogether too often, when I look around Richmond, Virginia, the racially divided former capital of the Confederacy and a city with one of the highest murder rates in the nation, the traces of reconciliation seem hard to find. Then again, the last time I saw white and black members of the city council engage in vigorous debate, reconciliation seemed at least possible. The last time I saw black and white fifth graders learning and playing together at Ginter Park Elementary School on Richmond's North Side, it almost looked easy.

The point is not that things actually are just fine, or that all injustice, much less all tragedy, has been vanquished. Things are not just fine. Injustice and tragedy are far from having been vanquished. The point is not that we are without legitimate reasons for pessimism, sorrow, and fear. We have our reasons. The point is rather that, in God's world as in God's church, there are occasions of grace. There are emergent possibilities for reconciling reconfigurations of human vision, devotion, and responsibility. Both world and church stand in need of reconciliation. Nevertheless, there are traces of grace, emergent possibilities for reconciliation and renewal in both church and world. Both church and world are racked by fragmentation and conflict. Nevertheless, and even where the forces of brokenness have done their worst, God resumes a society, God reestablishes a friendship that was threatened by dissolution and destruction.

MINISTRY, FAITH, AND HOPE

This, then, is the circumstance in which we undertake a ministry of reconciliation, and in this circumstance one important thing to say is that the ministry of reconciliation is realistic. It notes the corruptions and the tragedies, the grossly destructive violations that tear life's precious fabric, the chronic injustices that subvert life's dynamism. It is not surprised by persistent alienations and enmities. It is not surprised by the need for checks, balances, and restraints that sometimes help to deter egregious harm.

Another important thing to say is that the ministry of reconciliation tells us something important about the church. The church is the community and institution of those who acknowledge God's reconciling way with the world in Jesus Christ. It is the association of those who know that God's saving purpose is to overcome estrangement, alienation, and division by building up an all-inclusive community and commonwealth. It is the company of those who know that God is for the kingdom of God, and who therefore look for traces of God's reconciling grace even in unlikely places.[14]

As such, the church takes up an overarching task, both in its internal life and in its mission. It becomes the company of those who are loyal to God's cause and who attempt to put themselves at the service of true communion in community. It becomes an association whose purpose is to increase love of God and neighbor.[15] This is why it tries to resist temptations to turn in on itself and so betray the transformative event on which it depends. Testifying to God's inclusive and beloved community, the church tries to cross boundaries and to remain in communion with all of the many others in this fragmented and broken world. (And, as we know, altogether too often it fails.)

Nevertheless, another and an equally important thing to say is that God's reconciling work does not really depend on the church. It does not depend on our own righteousness and good character. It does not depend on our own powers and good abilities. In the words of Martin Luther's hymn, "did we in our own strength confide, our striving would be losing." Were it finally a matter of our own qualities and merits, as Methodists, Lutherans, Roman Catholics, Greek Orthodox, Presbyterians, evangelicals, liberals, Christians, or just plain people, the ministry of reconciliation would be hopeless.

The ministry of reconciliation is a work of faithful engagement. It is a work of loyalty and commitment to the cause of Jesus Christ. It is discipleship, an attempt to walk along a particular path. Indeed, the ministry of reconciliation has integrity and meaning precisely as it connects with the creation and renewal of a beloved community whose dimensions finally envelop every person and every community.[16] But the point of this ministry is not that the church brings about reconciliation by its own efforts. The point is not that the church brings about the beloved community by its own strength. The point is that we are entrusted with a message of reconciliation (2 Cor. 5:19). The point is to bear "a present witness to God's grace in Jesus Christ."[17] The point is to witness to what God is doing. The point is to announce a new possibility that, by the grace of God, is already breaking in, and in this sense is already present and available. The point is to point toward the traces of God's reconciling activity and to aid and abet the emergent possibilities that they bring for true communion in community.

To bear this witness is to respond faithfully to God's great reconciling work. It therefore means worship and outreach and care. It means compassion. It means joyful celebration and prophetic criticism. It means patience and daring. It means reflection and action. It means love and it means justice. It means repentance, and it even means the continual renewal of a social gospel.[18] But it does not mean that we bring in the kingdom by our own efforts, because the work of reconciliation is finally God's own work.

Clearly, there is much more to be said about the ministry of reconciliation. The historian may describe different ways in which Christian communities have understood it at different places and times. A sociologist may comment on the different social forms, from the hierarchical to the charismatic to the democratic, that our reconciling ministries may take. The analyst of ministerial leadership may show how different organizational forms in different circumstances favor different styles of management and administration. These are important and helpful things to say, and Christians and their churches do well to pay attention to them.

Theologically speaking, however, the more important point comes to us in a compelling image, a resonant bit of apostolic and reflective poetry. A strange thing has happened in the midst of our ecclesiastical and worldly conflicts and divisions. "In Christ *God* was reconciling the world to Godself." Despite our conflicts and divisions, this is why we may continue to receive the ministry of reconciliation in faith and in hope.

Notes

INTRODUCTION

1. Nathan Aviezer, *In the Beginning . . . Biblical Creation and Science* (Hoboken, N.J.: KTAV Publishing House, 1990), 15, 121.

2. Mireya Navarro, "Florida Case Highlights Conflicts on Use of Bible as a Textbook," *New York Times,* February 17, 1998, A-1, A-13.

3. W. A. Criswell, *Why I Preach That the Bible Is Literally True* (Nashville: Broadman Press, 1969), 95–118.

4. Ralph Wendell Burhoe, *Toward a Scientific Theology* (Belfast: Christian Journals Limited, 1981), 21–23, 196, 228. See also Willem Drees, *Religion, Science, and Naturalism* (Cambridge: Cambridge University Press, 1996), 223–24, and James M. Gustafson, *Ethics from a Theocentric Perspective,* vol. 1, *Theology and Ethics* (Chicago: University of Chicago Press, 1981), 252–54.

5. Consider the following quotation from Criswell, *Why I Preach That the Bible Is Literally True,* 94: "All truth is narrow. Mathematical truth is narrow. Two plus two equals four, no more, no less. . . . Scientific truth is narrow. There is no exception. Historical truth is narrow. An event happens at a certain place at a certain time in a certain way. . . . Geographical truth is narrow. . . . Ecclesiastical truth is no less narrow."

6. Thus, although I want to avoid a reductive literal-mindedness, I support attempts to achieve a broader intelligibility by engaging in conversations about theology and the findings of other disciplines. See Douglas F. Ottati, "Christian Theology and Other Disciplines," *Journal of Religion* 64, no. 2 (April 1984): 173–87; *Reforming Protestantism: Christian Commitment in Today's World* (Louisville: Westminster John Knox, 1995), chap. 3, 41–64; "Between Foundationalism and Nonfoundationalism," *Affirmation* 4, no. 2 (fall 1991): 27–47.

George A. Lindbeck's rather vague treatment of the question of truth comes in *The Nature of Doctrine: Religion and Theology in a Postliberal Age* (Philadelphia: Westminster Press, 1984), 63–69, and has been the subject of some important discussions. Among the more illuminating, I think, is Martin L. Cook, *The Open Circle: Confessional Methods in Theology* (Minneapolis: Fortress Press, 1991), 51–60. Cook notes that Lindbeck's work "lacks subtlety" when it comes to the connection between his own intratextual view of the world and the views generated by other, no less particular historical and social traditions. More recently some of Nancy Murphy's differences with Lindbeck stem from a similar judgment. See "Philosophical Resources for Postmodern Evangelical Theology," *Christian Scholar's Review,* 197–205. Cook also criticizes as "oversimplified" Paul Holmer's contention that "rationality is polymorphic" and different language-games are "incommensurable" (40–41). Years ago, so did I. See *Meaning and Method in H. Richard Niebuhr's Theology* (Washington, D.C.: University Press of America, 1982), 184–88.

7. Catherine Mowry LaCugna, *God For Us: The Trinity and Christian Life* (San Francisco: HarperSanFrancisco, 1991), 2. The nineteenth-century American theologian Horace Bushnell claimed that the Trinity is "a practical truth" because "it is nothing but the doctrine *that God is a being practically related to his creatures.*" See *Building Eras in Religion* (New York: Charles Scribner's Sons, 1903), 136.

8. See, for example, the metaphysically flattering editorial on my theology entitled "Turning Wine into Water" as well as other articles in *The Presbyterian Layman* 28, no. 5 (September–October, 1995). The editorial is on page 2.

1. Leadership-Speak in Contemporary Society

1. On the persistence of Social Darwinism, see Mary Midgley, *Beast and Man: The Animal Roots of Human Nature,* rev. ed. (London: Routledge, 1995), xiii–xxiii. Recently, E. J. Dionne Jr. has noted that "the new Republican philosophy looks *backward* to the late nineteenth century, seeking to revive the radical, unregulated capitalism of the Gilded Age and that era's belief that material progress depends on the fiercest forms of unchecked competition." See *They Only Look Dead: Why Progressives Will Dominate the Next Political Era* (New York: Simon & Schuster, 1996), 12.

2. Charles C. Manz and Henry P. Sims Jr., *Super-Leadership: Leading Others to Lead Themselves* (New York: Berkley Books, 1990), 71–79. Charles Slack, "Hoping for a Quick Takeoff: Airline's New Chief Executive Has Reputation as Tough, Aggressive Leader," *Richmond Times-Dispatch,* January 28, 1996, E-1, says that the head of the search committee that hired Stephen M. Wolf as USAir's chairman and CEO "compared Wolf to hockey great Wayne Gretzky." The article goes on to suggest that "a better sports analogy . . . might be Jimmy Johnson, the football coach who turned the mediocre Dallas Cowboys into Super Bowl champions."

3. During halftime of a football game last fall, a TV spot for one of the universities whose team was playing showed "leaders for tomorrow" being trained beneath a golden dome. Fortunately, a newsletter from my alma mater arrived the following

week to assure me that "leaders for the twenty-first century" are also being trained in Philadelphia.

4. *USAir Magazine,* vol. 3, no. 2 (February 1996). See an ad for Karros, The World Leader in Negotiating Programs, following p. 22. An ad on p. 7 for a software package called "ManagePro 3.1" says that it will help you "meet your goals and manage people better than ever before."

5. From an advertisement for Peter Lowe's Success 1996 in *Richmond Times Dispatch,* March 19, 1966, A-10. The specific session was offered by Dick Vitale.

6. Stuart R. Levine and Michael A. Crom, *The Leader in You: How to Win Friends, Influence People, and Succeed in a Changing World* (New York: Simon & Schuster, 1993). Manz and Sims, *Super-Leadership.*

7. Alasdair MacIntyre, *After Virtue: A Study in Moral Theory* (Notre Dame, Ind.: University of Notre Dame Press, 1981), 70–75.

8. George S. Odiorne, *How Managers Make Things Happen,* 2d ed. (Englewood Cliffs, N.J.: Prentice-Hall, 1987), 23, 80. See also Levine and Crom, *The Leader in You,* 15.

9. See, for example, Manz and Sims, *Super-Leadership,* 70, 80.

10. Odiorne, *How Managers Make Things Happen,* 143–44, 146.

11. Manz and Sims, *Super-Leadership,* 110–34; Odiorne, *How Managers Make Things Happen,* 23, 30.

12. Hyrum Smith, *The Ten Natural Laws of Successful Time and Life Management: Proven Strategies for Increased Productivity and Inner Peace* (New York: Warner Books, 1994), 7, 129, 214, 217.

13. Robert Heilbroner and William Milberg make similar points about the modern study of economics in *The Crisis of Vision in Modern Economic Thought* (New York: Cambridge University Press, 1995). They argue that economics is best understood as a study deeply immersed in history, and they emphasize the importance of a pre-analytic grasp of the central issues in each period that economics is meant to address. These points are brought out by Richard Parker in "The Monetary Science: A Review of *The Crisis of Vision in Modern Economic Thought,*" *New York Times Book Review,* January 28, 1996, 29. Paul Tillich notes that "technical reasoning" asks about means to ends but not about which ends are appropriate or good. See his *Systematic Theology* (Chicago: University of Chicago Press, 1959), vol. 1, 71–75.

14. See, for example, Bill Parcells, "Finding a Way to Win," *USAir Magazine,* vol. 3, no. 2 (February 1996): 14–18. The article is an excerpt from *Finding a Way to Win* by Bill Parcells with Jeff Coplon (New York: Doubleday, 1995).

15. M. Scott Peck, *The Road Less Traveled: A New Psychology of Love, Traditional Values, and Spiritual Growth* (New York: Simon & Schuster, 1978), 168.

16. See note 15 above.

17. Diane Dreher, *The Tao of Personal Leadership* (San Francisco: HarperBusiness, 1997).

18. Laurie Beth Jones, *Jesus CEO: Using Ancient Wisdom for Visionary Leadership* (New York: Hyperion, 1995), 125, 178–79.

19. Ibid., xiv–xv, 39–42, 65–67, 186–89, 200, 201.

20. Bruce Barton, *The Man Nobody Knows: A Discovery of the Real Jesus* (Indianapolis: Bobbs-Merrill, 1924, 1925), 23. The word in brackets is mine.

21. Ibid., n.p.

22. Ibid., 162. Bracketed words are mine. Business emphasis is Barton's.

23. Ibid., 177. Deepak Chopra, a contemporary who draws on Indian and other Eastern themes, comes closer to undermining the leader-manager when he says that

"there are many aspects to success; material wealth is only one component." He also writes of the laws of "least effort" and "detachment" in ways that most mainstream and competitive leader-managers would find it difficult to accept. On the other hand, Chopra does not entirely leave behind a certain striving for material wealth. "If you put your attention on these laws and practice the steps outlined in this book, you will see that you can manifest anything you want—all the affluence, money, and success that you desire." See *The Seven Spiritual Laws of Success: A Practical Guide to the Fulfillment of Your Dreams* (San Rafael, Calif.: Amber-Allen Publishing, 1994), 2, 109.

24. This is not unlike the way John Dewey writes about art and the aesthetic in *Art as Experience* (New York: Milton, Balch & Company, 1934), 195.

25. Cora Diamond, "The Importance of Being Human," Royal Institute of Philosophy Supplement: 29, *Human Beings,* ed. David Cockburn (Cambridge: Cambridge University Press, 1991), 49–50.

26. Ibid., 49–50.

27. Hans Jonas, *The Imperative of Responsibility* (Chicago: University of Chicago Press, 1984), 27.

28. Stephen E. Ambrose, *Eisenhower: Soldier and President* (New York: Simon & Schuster, 1990), 129.

29. *Collected Papers of Charles Saunders Peirce,* ed. Charles Hartshorne and Paul Weiss (Cambridge: Belknap Press of Harvard University Press, 1978), VI: 313, 314.

30. See James M. Gustafson, *Ethics from a Theocentric Perspective,* vol. 1, *Theology and Ethics* (Chicago: University of Chicago Press, 1981), 281–84.

31. See Ambrose, *Eisenhower,* 120–41.

32. See "Weapons of the Spirit," a videorecording produced, written, and directed by Pierre Sauvage (New York: First Run/Icarus Films, 1988), 91 min. Le Chambon-sur-Lignon is a Protestant village that took in and sheltered 5000 Jews. Sauvage himself was born and protected there.

33. See Taylor Branch's closing comments about Martin Luther King Jr., race, and nonviolence in *The Parting of the Waters: America in the King Years 1954–63* (New York: Simon & Schuster, 1988), 922. I should add that, if you haven't been to the National Civil Rights Museum in Memphis, Tennessee, you might think about going. Few experiences are more moving than walking up a ramp past photographs and displays of the civil rights movement to find that one has ascended to rooms 306 and 307 of the Lorraine Motel. The spot on the balcony where King was shot is marked by a wreath of flowers.

2. Envisioning God and Ourselves

1. Friedrich Schleiermacher, *The Christian Faith,* ed. H. R. Macintosh and J. S. Stewart (Philadelphia: Fortress Press, 1976), 1–2.

2. Gordon D. Kaufman noted current confusion in *An Essay on Theological Method* (Missoula, Mont.: Scholars Press, 1979), ix, 1. If anything, the theological scene has become more confusing since he wrote.

3. To some extent and degree, human life is almost always a matter of interpretive envisioning. This is so because, in our many interactions with our social and natural environments, we find ourselves confronted with virtually countless persons, things, causes, and communities which vie for our attention and devotion, as well as by many interdependent relations of responsibility and trust. We therefore also find ourselves in need of ways of selecting, organizing, and prioritizing. We find ourselves in need of interactive orientations or ways of negotiating life. These are furnished by

our particular communities and their heritages, and they entail visions or strong readings of the many situations and realities with which we interact. Or, again, we might say that our human circumstance does not simply and intelligibly arrange itself. We need to bring images, ideas, and patterns to bear on our experiences if we are to make sense of them. Our communities and their heritages furnish images, ideas, and patterns that enable us to make sense by constructing interpretative visions. These sense-making and poetic visions, in turn, are fundamental for our practical stances or ways of negotiating life. I discuss these assumptions in more detail in *Reforming Protestantism: Christian Commitment in Today's World* (Louisville: Westminster John Knox, 1995), 41–64.

4. Of course, within each broad religious movement, there are also important subcommunities and subtraditions. For example, Reformed theology is a specific sort of Christian theology. It is a particular pattern of Christian convictional wisdom about God and ourselves that is borne by Reformed Christian communities and their particular Christian subtradition. Similar things might be said about Methodist theology, Greek Orthodox theology, and so on. I comment on some challenges and possibilities presented by the plurality of religious movements and subtraditions in chapter 5, "Table Conversation."

The work of theological envisioning amounts to a "seeing as" rather than a detached or neutral description. This is one reason why it is a mistake to impose standards of constraining proof or geometric demonstration on theological inquiry. (Richard B. Miller makes a similar point about practical reasoning and casuistry in *Casuistry and Modern Ethics: A Poetics of Practical Reasoning* (Chicago: University of Chicago Press, 1996), 223–28.) Nevertheless, as it involves sorting through an immense and multifaceted treasury of artifacts and activities, identifying important symbols and patterns, and bringing these to bear on our experiences, theological inquiry is reflective in a variety of senses. It is exegetical because it entails continuous and disciplined reflections on the scriptures, or classic literary expressions of the initial stages of the Christian movement. It is traditional because it involves reflections on subsequent practices and expressions of the historical movement whose life is informed by the scriptural charter documents. In addition, Christian theology is reasonable because both exegesis and the interpretation of tradition are works of logic and imagination. It is also reasonable in the sense that a theologian tries to link together the many symbols, images, and ideas of the church's poetry. She or he tries to show how they are related to one another, how they "hang together" in a self-consistent scheme. Again, the theologian articulates an interpretation of human life and the world which interprets relatively common situations and realities that other persons and communities also interpret in the light of other aims, symbols, and ideas. Christian theology is reflective in the sense that it offers a poetic vision of things in their appropriate interrelations with God and one another which can and should be brought into conversation with other interpretations and visions.

See also Douglas F. Ottati, *Jesus Christ and Christian Vision* (Louisville: Westminster John Knox, 1995), 13–15. These points of reference (scripture, tradition, reason, and experience) signal broad standards of judgment in theological reflection. A Christian theologian tries to develop central themes and symbols in a manner that is both informed by and adequate to scripture and tradition. She tries to render a theological vision that protects the integrity of Christian faith. At the same time, a Christian theologian tries to render a coherent theological vision that engages other, equally particular interpretations and construals of objects, situations, and realities that are offered by other persons and communities. These engagements may lead her to criticize and reject an alternative interpretative vision, but they may also lead her to recast, revise, and enhance her interpretation of things in relation to God. In these ways, a Christian theologian tries to render a theological vision that is comprehensible or intelligible in the sense of being responsive to interpretations offered by other persons and communities. I develop the standards of integrity and intelligibility for theological inquiry in *Meaning and Method in H. Richard Niebuhr's Theology* (Washington, D.C.: University Press of America, 1982). I give further account of these standards with respect to different types of theology and in conversation with philosophy of science in "Between Foundationalism and Nonfoundationalism," *Affirmation* 4, no. 2 (fall 1991): 27–47.

5. My claim that Christian theology aims at an appropriate degree of definiteness differs from Schleiermacher's contention that, in dogmatics, we should aim at "the highest degree of definiteness." *The Christian Faith,* 78–83. By and large, I do not believe that Christian theology either can or should frame a dialectically correct discourse that leaves behind figurative expressions, poetic and rhetorical language. I prefer the more energetic and sermonic language of John Calvin's *Institutes of the Christian Religion.*

On language, piety, and system in Calvin and in Schleiermacher, see B. A. Gerrish, "Theology within the Limits of Piety Alone: Schleiermacher and Calvin's Notion of God," *The Old Protestantism and the New: Essays on the Reformation Heritage* (Chicago: University of Chicago Press, 1982), 196–207, and *Grace and Gratitude: The Eucharistic Theology of John Calvin* (Minneapolis: Fortress Press, 1993), 14–19, 50–52. Calvin certainly cares for orderliness, systematic coherence, and interconnection. But Gerrish rightly notes a difficulty that attends figurative language in theology, namely, an occasional inexactitude and imprecision.

6. See H. Richard Niebuhr, *Theology, History, and Culture: Major Unpublished Writings,* ed. William Stacy Johnson (New Haven, Conn.: Yale University Press, 1995), 19–33.

7. George Steiner, *Real Presences* (Chicago: University of Chicago Press, 1991), 227.

8. Julian N. Hartt, *Theological Method and Imagination* (New York: Seabury Press, 1977), 77.

9. On my understanding of tradition, see *Jesus Christ and Christian Vision,* 1–15.

10. Robert Frost says something similar about a poem in "The Figure a Poem Makes," *Collected Poems of Robert Frost, 1939* (New York: Henry Holt and Company, 1944).

11. I think John Calvin was simply right about this in his inspired opening sentence of his *Institutes of the Christian Religion,* ed. John T. McNeill, trans. Ford Lewis Battles (Philadelphia: Westminster Press, 1960), I, i, 1. "Nearly all the wisdom we possess, that is to say, true and sound wisdom, consists of two parts: the knowledge of God and of ourselves." H. Richard Niebuhr claimed that "the object of that whole series of inquiries we call theology is always man before God and God before man." See *Theology, History, and Culture,* 80.

12. Paul Ricoeur, *Interpretation Theory: Discourse and the Surplus of Meaning* (Fort Worth: Texas Christian University Press, 1976), 67.

13. Nathan Scott Jr., *The Broken Center: Studies in the Theological Horizon of Modern Literature* (New Haven, Conn.: Yale University Press, 1966), 177.

14. George Steiner speaks of the covenant between word and world, and claims that the breaking of this covenant in Western history defines modernity. See *Real Presences,* 93, 97–98, 105.

15. William Schweiker notes that the modern Western moral outlook pivots on "the metaphysical proposition that humans are the only agents in the world," and he links this with the story of the Tower of Babel. See "Power and the Agency of God," *Theology Today* 52, no. 2 (1995): 204–24.

16. This is substantially James M. Gustafson's position in *Ethics from a Theocentric Perspecive,* vol. 1, *Theology and Ethics* (Chicago: University of Chicago Press, 1981), 235–51.

17. More than a little narrative theology falls into the first trap. Gordon D. Kaufman's theology as imaginative construction falls into the second. See Hans W. Frei, *The Eclipse of the Biblical Narrative: A Study in Eighteenth and Nineteenth Century Hermeneutics* (New Haven, Conn.: Yale University Press, 1974), 13–16; William C. Placher, *Unapologetic Theology: A Christian Voice in a Pluralistic Conversation* (Louisville: Westminster/John Knox, 1989), 123–35; Gordon D. Kaufman, *God—Mystery—Diversity: Christian Theology in a Pluralistic World* (Minneapolis: Fortress Press, 1996), 1–12, 96–109.

18. I write about sin and original sin in more detail in *Reforming Protestantism,* 66–73.

19. I think that Gerhard von Rad's section on this in his *Old Testament Theology,* vol. I, *The Theology of Israel's Historical Traditions,* trans. D. M. G. Stalker (New York: Harper & Row, 1962), 136–65, is still a classic of theological literature.

20. James M. Gustafson argues that the classic symbols of God as Creator, Sustainer and Governor, Judge, and Redeemer both express and interpret patterns in our experience in the world. See *Ethics from a Theocentric Perspective,* vol. 1, *Theology and Ethics,* 235–51.

21. Cornelius Plantinga Jr., *Not the Way It's Supposed to Be: A Breviary of Sin* (Grand Rapids, Mich.: Eerdmans, 1995), 6, points out that, in the Christian view, "sin is not an independent entity or topic." It has to be framed by creation and redemption. My point is similar, although, as I shall hasten to add, each of the major Christian symbols needs to be framed by all of the others.

22. What I say here owes a great deal to Claus Westermann, *Creation* (Philadelphia: Fortress Press, 1971), 39–65, and also James M. Gustafson, *Ethics from a Theocentric Perspective,* vol. 1, *Theology and Ethics,* 236–8, 281–93.

23. Calvin, *Institutes,* II, i, 10.

24. Calvin, *Institutes,* I, xiv, 1.

25. Among earlier theologians typical illustrations of wicked actions and plans "overruled for good" include the conduct of Joseph's brothers, the obstinacy of Pharaoh, and the crucifixion. See Charles Hodge, *Systematic Theology,* vol. 1 (Grand Rapids, Mich.: Eerdmans, 1977), 590. Some theologians virtually equate creation and providence, and it is easy to see why, since providence may be regarded as a continuation of God's ordering and upholding of all creation. But this misses the "despite sin's corruption" aspect of God's continuing and sustaining governance. Providence means the continuation of God's dependable faithfulness despite the world's corruption. Along these lines, I think of God's covenant with Noah and all other creatures as a quintessential expression of providence, and here I cannot help quoting one of my favorite lines from scripture. "This is the sign of the covenant that I make between me and you and every living creature that is with you, for all future generations: I have set my bow in the clouds . . ." (Genesis 9:12–13a).

26. I discuss redeeming grace in more detail in *Reforming Protestantism,* 80–86.

27. I make this point in greater detail in *Reforming Protestantism,* 23–40.

3. The Sense the Trinity Makes

1. So much so, in fact, that John Calvin could wish that a good many trinitarian terms were buried if only we would avoid false teaching. *Institutes of the Christian Religion,* trans. Ford Lewis Battles, ed. John T. McNeill (Philadelphia: Westminster Press, 1960), I, xiii, 5.

2. Catherine LaCugna, *God for Us: The Trinity and Christian Life* (San Francisco: HarperSanFrancisco, 1991), 2.

3. Horace Bushnell said that the Trinity is "a practical truth" because "it is nothing but the doctrine *that God is a being practically related to his creatures."* See *Building Eras in Religion* (New York: Charles Scribner's Sons, 1903), 136.

4. I comment on the turn from local creeds to those adopted by authoritative councils in *Jesus Christ and Christian Vision* (Louisville: Westminster John Knox, 1995), 20–26.

5. *Harper's Bible Dictionary,* Paul J. Achtemeier, gen. ed. (San Francisco: Harper & Row Publishers, 1985), 401.

6. Carole R. Fontaine, "Proverbs," *The Women's Bible Commentary,* ed. Carol A. Newsom and Sharon H. Ringe (Louisville: Westminster John Knox, 1992), 146–48.

7. Jaroslav Pelikan, *The Christian Tradition: A History of the Development of Doctrine,* vol. 1, *The Emergence of the Catholic Tradition (100–600)* (Chicago: University of Chicago Press, 1971), 73.

8. H. Richard Niebuhr, *Radical Monotheism and Western Culture with Supplementary Essays* (Louisville: Westminster John Knox, 1993), 31–37.

9. Paul Tillich, *The Courage to Be* (New Haven, Conn.: Yale University Press, 1952).

10. H. Richard Niebuhr, *The Responsible Self: An Essay in Christian Moral Philosophy* (New York: Harper & Row, 1963), 177.

11. "A Brief Statement of Faith," *The Constitution of the Presbyterian Church (U.S.A.): Part I, The Book of Confessions* (Louisville: Office of the General Assembly, 1994), 10.4 (p. 276).

12. Much that I say here is said in more detail by H. Richard Niebuhr in "The Doctrine of the Trinity and the Unity of the Church," *Theology, History, and Culture: Major Unpublished Writings,* ed. William Stacy Johnson (New Haven, Conn.: Yale University Press, 1995), 52–62.

13. I interpret the Trinity as a symbolization of both plurality and unity in the Christian community's discernment of God in *Jesus Christ and Christian Vision,* 103–6, 138–40.

14. Karl Rahner, *The Trinity,* trans. Joseph Donceel (New York: Seabury Press, 1974), 22.

15. The most elegant statement of this point by a Christian theologian is surely Jonathan Edwards's "Dissertation Concerning the End for which God Created the World" in *The Works of Jonathan Edwards,* vol. 8, *Ethical Writings,* ed. Paul Ramsey (New Haven, Conn.: Yale University Press, 1989), 428–63, 526–36.

16. Johannes Wollebius, Compendium Theologiae Christianae in *Reformed Dogmatics: Seventeenth-Century Reformed Theology Through the Writings of Wollebius, Voetius, and Turretin,* ed. John W. Beardslee III (Grand Rapids, Mich.: Baker Book House, 1977), 37.

17. Calvin, *Institutes,* I, xv, 4. "For that speculation of Augustine, that the soul is the reflection of the Trinity because in it reside the understanding, will, and memory, is by no means sound."

18. The incomprehensibility of God is a point associated in recent theology with Karl Rahner and his work on Thomas Aquinas. See Karl Rahner, *Foundations of Christian Faith: An Introduction to the Idea of Christianity* (New York: Seabury Press, A Crossroad Book, 1978), 75–89, 454–56. But the notion is also found elsewhere. For example, commenting on the Trinity, Calvin pens the following admonition in his *Institutes,* I, xiii, 21:

> Here, indeed, if anywhere in the secret mysteries of Scripture, we ought to play the philosopher soberly and with great moderation; let us use great caution that neither our thoughts nor our speech go beyond the limits to which the Word of God itself extends. For how can the human mind measure off the measureless essence of God according to its own little measure, a mind as yet unable to establish for certain the nature of the sun's body, though men's eyes daily gaze upon it? Indeed, how can the mind by its own leading come to search out God's essence when it cannot even get at its own? Let us then willingly leave to God the knowledge of himself.

Again, the Scots Confession of 1560 is quick to assert that God "is eternal, infinite, immeasurable, incomprehensible, omnipotent, invisible," a point on which it is joined by the Westminster Confession of Faith. See *The Constitution of the Presbyterian Church (U.S.A.), Part I: Book of Confessions* (Louisville: Office of the General Assembly, 1994), 3.01 (p. 11), 6.011 (p. 128).

On related points concerning the hiddenness of God, see chapter 5, "Table Conversation."

19. Rosemary Radford Ruether, *Sexism and God-Talk: Toward a Feminist Theology* (Boston: Beacon Press, 1983), 68–69, 66–67. Or, again, "Insofar as we use gender images metaphorically for God, we must do so in a way that clearly reveals them as metaphorical, not literal." Rosemary Radford Ruether, "Christian Anthropology and Gender: A Tribute to Jürgen Moltmann," *The Future of Theology: Essays in Honor of Jürgen Moltmann,* ed. Miroslave Wolf, Carmen Kreig, and Thomas Kucharz (Grand Rapids, Mich.: Eerdmans, 1996), 252.

4. Meaning and Mystery of Resurrection

1. See also my shorter piece, "Meditation on Easter Sunday," *The Presbyterian Outlook* (April 1, 1997): 5–7.

2. Kenneth L. Woodward, "Rethinking the Resurrection," *Newsweek,* April 8, 1996, 61–70.

3. Gustavo Gutiérrez, *A Theology of Liberation: History, Politics, and Salvation,* 15th anniv. ed., revised, with a new introduction, trans. Sister Caridad Inda and John Eagleston (Maryknoll, N.Y.: Orbis Books, 1988), 100–101, 103.

4. For a fuller discussion of these and related points about sin, see Douglas F. Ottati, *Reforming Protestantism: Christian Commitment in Today's World* (Louisville: Westminster John Knox, 1995), 65–91.

5. For further elaboration of these points, see Douglas F. Ottati, *Jesus Christ and Christian Vision* (Louisville: Westminster John Knox, 1995), 73–95.

6. *The Constitution of the Presbyterian Church (U.S.A.): Part I, The Book of Confessions* (Louisville: The Office of the General Assembly, 1994), 4.001 (p. 29). Hereafter cited BOC, 4.001 (p. 29).

7. As is well known, John Calvin organized the 1559 edition of his *Institutes of the Christian Religion* around themes of knowledge of God the Creator and knowledge of God the Redeemer. He claimed that faith is "a firm and certain knowledge of God's benevolence toward us, founded upon the truth of the freely given promise in Christ." *Institutes of the Christian Religion,* trans. Ford Lewis Battles, ed. John T. McNeill (Philadelphia: Westminster Press, 1960), III, ii, 7.

8. Jonathan Edwards, *A History of the Work of Redemption,* ed. John F. Wilson, vol. 9, *The Works of Jonathan Edwards,* John E. Smith, gen. ed. (New Haven, Conn.: Yale University Press, 1989), 100.

9. The term "cosmic optimism" was used by Perry Miller to describe elements of Puritan piety in *The New England Mind: The Seventeenth Century* (Boston: Beacon Press, 1961), 18. "Also in the interests of consistency, the Puritans were led to a further deduction: if the creation is ruled by God's will, and His will is itself the norm of justice and equity, the universe must be essentially good. They may be described as cosmic optimists."

10. H. Richard Niebuhr, *Faith on Earth: An Enquiry into the Structure of Human Faith,* ed. Richard R. Niebuhr (New Haven, Conn.: Yale University Press, 1989), 100.

11. BOC, 7.001 (p. 181).

12. Jonathan Edwards, "Charity and Its Fruits," in *Ethical Writings,* ed. Paul Ramsey, vol. 8, *The Works of Jonathan Edwards,* John E. Smith, gen. ed. (New Haven, Conn.: Yale University Press, 1989), 366–97.

13. *H. Richard Niebuhr: Theology, History, and Culture,* ed. William Stacy Johnson (New Haven, Conn.: Yale University Press, 1996), 128.

14. Joseph A. Fitzmyer, *The Gospel According to Luke, X–XXIV* (Garden City, N.Y.: Doubleday, 1985), 1533–38.

15. Carolyn Walker Bynum, *The Resurrection of the Body in Western Christianity, 200–1336* (New York: Columbia University Press, 1995), 4, 6. See also Hans Cönzelmann, *1 Corinthians: A Commentary on the First Epistle to the Corinthians,* trans. James W. Leitch (Philadelphia: Fortress Press, 1975), 281–83; Joseph A. Fitzmyer, S.J., *The Gospel According to Luke,* X-XXIV, 1539.

16. Karl Barth, *Church Dogmatics* (Edinburgh: T. & T. Clark, 1968), 3/2:451–53.

17. Emil Brunner, *The Christian Doctrine of Creation and Redemption,* vol. 2 of *Dogmatics,* trans. Olive Wyon (Philadelphia: Westminster Press, 1952), 371.

18. Ibid., 371–72.

19. Ibid., 372.

20. Rudolf Bultmann, *Faith and Understanding,* ed. Robert W. Funk (Minneapolis: Fortress Press, 1987), 177.

21. Rudolf Bultmann et al., *Kerygma and Myth: A Theological Debate,* ed. Hans Werner Bartsch (New York: Harper & Row, 1961), 41.

22. Ibid., 42.

23. Willi Marxsen, *The Resurrection of Jesus of Nazareth* (Philadelphia: Fortress Press, 1970), 138–41.

24. Peter C. Hodgson, *Jesus—Word and Presence: An Essay in Christology* (Philadelphia: Fortress Press, 1971), 231–32.

25. Peter C. Hodgson, *Winds of the Spirit: A Constructive Christian Theology* (Louisville: Westminster/John Knox, 1994), 264–74.

26. Stephen T. Davis, *Risen Indeed: Making Sense of the Resurrection* (Grand Rapids, Mich.: Eerdmans, 1993), 58–59.

27. John Shelby Spong, *Resurrection: Myth or Reality? A Bishop's Search for the Origins of Christianity* (San Francisco: HarperSanFrancisco, 1994), 259–60.

28. John Hick, *The Metaphor of God Incarnate: Christology in a Pluralistic Age* (Louisville: Westminster/John Knox, 1993), 23.

29. Ibid., 24; "Jesus and the World Religions," *The Myth of God Incarnate,* ed. John Hick (Philadelphia: Westminster Press, 1977), 170.

30. Hick, *The Metaphor of God Incarnate,* 24–25.

31. My remarks here parallel John Calvin's understanding of Christ's real spiritual presence in the sacrament of the Eucharist. See chapter 5, "Table Conversation."

32. Many people think it important to call the resurrection an event, and I do not disagree. However, I also think that, when we are not careful, event-language makes for difficulties. This is because some use it to invest Jesus' resurrection with an "objectivity" that can be sharply distinguished from a "merely subjective" and intra-psychic experience. But this begs the question of just what there was that was independent of the subjectivities of the persons and groups to whom the risen Christ appeared. And, the New Testament is not very helpful on this point, as it always portrays the risen Christ in connection with the experiences of the faithful.

Perhaps we should say that the "something" independent of the subjectivities of those to whom he appeared was a physical body of Jesus that took up space, could be seen and touched by anyone under certain conditions, etc. Yet, as we have seen, while such a specification of the "objective event" accords with some appearance narratives in the New Testament, it does not accord very well with others. Despite some of Davis's arguments, it also seems difficult to know just how fully such a specification accords with Paul's discussion in 1 Corinthians 15.

It is sometimes said that people must believe in a physical bodily resurrection, or else they are not Christian, not saved, not faithful, or what have you. This, after all, is the clearest way to insist on the importance of an objective event. But it not only turns faith into a work (of credulity); it also threatens to cast aside some of the writers of scripture itself.

I think it is worth asking whether strict distinctions between the "merely subjective" and the "truly objective" are especially helpful. Take the accounts in Acts of Paul's experience of the risen Christ on the Damascus road. Is it "truly objective" or "merely subjective"? Remember it is unclear what Paul sees and those travelling with him are variously portrayed as only hearing the voice or only seeing the light.

Event-language can be helpful if we do not insist on strict objective-subjective dichotomies. Then it may be used to say that there is an occurrence which gives rise to the resurrection symbol and narratives of the New Testament. But when used in this way, event-language does not tell us whether this occurrence is a series of bodily appearances, or the emergence of a vision of Jesus alive among his disciples.

33. This is the first sentence of "A Brief Statement of Faith" that was adopted into *The Book of Confessions* by the Presbyterian Church (U.S.A.) in 1992. See BOC, 10.1 (p. 275). It picks up prominent themes of Romans 14:7–9 and John Calvin's summary of the Christian life as well as the first question of the Heidelberg Catechism. In his *Institutes,* III, vii, 1, Calvin notes that we are not our own. Then he writes, "Conversely, we are God's: let us therefore live for him and die for him." Question 1 of the Heidelberg Catechism in BOC, 4.001 (p. 29) begins as follows. "What is your only comfort, in life and in death? A. That I belong—body and soul, in life and in death—not to myself but to my faithful Savior, Jesus Christ . . ."

5. Table Conversation

1. Ulrich Zwingli, *Commentary on True and False Religion* (Durham, N.C.: The Labyrinth Press, 1981), 201, 205, 216, 229, 233, 237–38.

2. *Luther's Works,* vol. 36, *Word and Sacrament II,* ed. Abdel Ross Wentz (Philadelphia: Muhlenberg Press, 1959), 335; *Luther's Works,* vol. 37, *Word and Sacrament III,* ed. Robert H. Fischer (Philadelphia: Muhlenberg Press, 1961), 51, 53.

3. *Luther's Works,* vol. 37, *Word and Sacrament III,* 64. Eberhard Grötzinger argues that the differences between Luther and Zwingli go back to their criticisms of the medieval mass. *Luther und Zwingli: Die Kritik an der mittelalterlichen Lehre von der Messe—als Wurzel des Abendsmahlsstreites* (Zürich: Benziger Verlag, 1980), 119–21.

4. John Calvin, *Institutes of the Christian Religion,* trans. Ford Lewis Battles, ed. John T. McNeill (Philadelphia: Westminster Press,1960), IV, xvii, 5, 10, 12, 30, 36. My interpretation of Calvin follows B. A. Gerrish, *Grace and Gratitude: The Eucharistic Theology of John Calvin* (Minneapolis: Fortress Press, 1993), 157–82. E. David Willis notes that the Lutherans regarded Calvin's position as "only another watering down of Christ's explicit words." See *Calvin's Catholic Christology: The Function of the So-Called Extra Calvinisticum in Calvin's Theology* (Leiden: E. J. Brill, 1966), 14. Jaroslav Pelikan calls the doctrine of the real presence in the eucharist "the principal dogmatic difference setting Lutheranism apart from Calvinism." *The Christian Tradition: A History of the Development of Doctrine,* vol. 4: *Reformation of Church and Dogma (1300–1700)* (Chicago: University of Chicago Press, 1984), 352.

5. E. David Willis, *Calvin's Catholic Christology,* 9–10. Calvin himself rejected "the monstrous notion of ubiquity." See *Institutes,* IV, xvii, 30.

6. *The Book of Concord: The Confessions of the Evangelical Lutheran Church,* trans. Theodore G. Tappert (Philadelphia: Muhlenberg Press, 1959), 489.

7. Frances Turretin, *Institutes of Elenctic Theology,* trans. George Musgrave Giger (Phillipsburg, N.J.: Presbyterian and Reformed Publishing Co., 1992), vol. 2, 323–27.

8. Karl-Heinz Zur Mühlen, "Christology," *Oxford Encyclopedia of the Reformation,* ed. Hans J. Hillerbrand (New York: Oxford University Press, 1996), vol. 1, 315.

9. Calvin, *Institutes,* II, xiii, 4.

10. Heiko Augustus Oberman, *The Dawn of the Reformation: Essays in Later Medieval and Early Reformation Thought* (Edinburgh: T. & T. Clark, 1986), 239, 247. E. David Willis notes that the term was probably introduced during the 1620s. See *Calvin's Catholic Christology,* 9, 23.

11. See Pelikan, *The Christian Tradition,* vol. 1, 353–54. Strident polemics eventually found their way to North America. The Presbyterian, Charles Hodge, regarded Lutheran doctrine as a patchwork of contradictions that confuses the infinite and the finite and "destroys the integrity of the human nature of Christ." *Systematic Theology* (Grand Rapids, Mich.: Eerdmans, 1977), vol. 2, 416, 418. Partly in response, the Missouri Synod Lutheran, Francis Pieper, claimed that Reformed Christology is highly inconsistent and that it has both un-Christian and Christian aspects. When it follows rationalistic axioms, says Pieper, Reformed theology "destroys the foundation of the Christian faith." *Christian Dogmatics* (St. Louis: Concordia Publishing House, 1951), 271, 279.

12. Oberman, *Dawn of the Reformation,* 257–58.

13. I. A. Dorner suggests that the Reformed and Lutheran Christologies betray distinct religious motives or pieties. See *History of the Development of the Doctrine of the Person of Christ,* trans. D. W. Simon (Edinburgh: T. & T. Clark, 1862), Division II,

vol. II, 136–38; *A System of Christian Doctrine,* trans. Alfred Cave and J. S. Banks (Edinburgh: T. & T. Clark, 1882), vol. III, 242–43.

14. The Reformed theologian Donald G. Bloesch recently has made this claim. See *Essentials of Evangelical Theology* (New York: Harper & Row, 1982), vol. 1, 134. Francis Pieper criticized Reformed theology for adhering to this and other "rationalistic axioms." See *Christian Dogmatics,* 271–79.

15. Oberman, *Dawn of the Reformation,* 253–54.

16. Barth, *Church Dogmatics,* 1/2:169–70. Maresius is quoted by Heinrich Heppe, *Reformed Dogmatics Set Out and Illustrated from the Original Sources,* trans. G. T. Thompson (Grand Rapids, Mich.: Baker Book House, 1978), 418. I. A. Dorner also gives a rather complete explanation of the Reformed doctrine in *A System of Christian Doctrine,* vol. III, 241. The Logos, he writes, "also eternally is and remains omnipresently active outside the humanity and its limitation. Since the humanity must remain finite, the infinite Logos could never be *totaliter in carne.* It is . . . everywhere wholly, and therefore also *totus in carne* of Christ. But it is also *extra carnem,* and remains so."

17. Barth, *Church Dogmatics,* 1/2:169.

18. He therefore concludes that, rather than an *extra calvinisticum,* it would be more appropriate to speak of an *extra catholicum* or an *extra patristicum.* See *Calvin's Catholic Theology,* 60. Thomas Aquinas insisted that "the infinite is never fully fathomed by the finite." And, he went on to write that "Although the entire divine nature was united to human nature in the one person of the Son, the whole power of the divinity was not as it were circumscribed by that human nature. As Augustine writes, *I want you to know that Christian doctrine does not hold that God became so involved with flesh that he deserted or put aside the task of governing the universe, or that he transferred it, confined and constricted, within that meagre body." Summa Theologiae,* Thomas Gilby, gen. ed. (New York: Blackfriars in conjunction with McGraw-Hill Book Company, 1974), 3a, 10, 1.

19. For further elaborations of some of the ideas presented under this thesis, see my book, *Jesus Christ and Christian Vision* (Louisville: Westminster John Knox, 1995), 16–49, 131–34.

20. Calvin, *Institutes,* II, viii, 1; IV, xx, 16. See also Willis, *Calvin's Catholic Christology,* 109–10, 143–47, 151–52.

21. H. Richard Niebuhr, *The Purpose of the Church and Its Ministry: Reflections on the Aims of Theological Education* (New York: Harper & Row, 1956), 44–46.

22. Let me also mention a speculative question. Suppose there are intelligent beings on a planet in another galaxy thousands of light-years from earth. Even if we launch a spacecraft with a Bible in it now, countless generations will rise and fall without knowing Jesus. Can they know God? In answering, we need not choose between the geocentric insistence that life-forms which do not know Jesus of Nazareth are simply beyond the pale and relativistic claims that the knowledge of God available to different life-forms is wholly incommensurable. Another option is that the communicative activity of the God who comes to us in Jesus Christ extends also beyond Jesus of Nazareth and, indeed, encompasses all planets and all galaxies.

23. John Calvin, *The Gospel According to St. John: Part One,* volume 4 of *Calvin's New Testament Commentaries* (Grand Rapids, Mich.: Eerdmans, 1974), 7, 20–1.

24. See James M. Gustafson's discussion of this and related themes in *A Sense of the Divine: The Natural Environment from a Theocentric Perspective* (Cleveland: Pilgrim Press, 1994). Among other things, Gustafson notes that, for Calvin, humans have a sense of

the divine through the powers of nature (p. 45). Rosemary Radford Ruether's *Gaia and God: An Ecofeminist Theology of Earth Healing* (San Francisco: HarperSanFrancisco, 1992) explores how a number of traditional images and themes stress the presence of deity in creation. Some years ago, Joseph Sittler wrote that "the Christian doctrine of redemption stands alongside of the Christian doctrine of creation," and that together they point to the reality of God working itself out in the world-as-nature and the world-as-history. He noted that "if there is postulated a logos-toward-redemption at work in history, and if the Lord who is disclosed there is postulated as the Lord of all that is, then this same comprehensiveness must inhere in an adequate Christology." *Essays on Nature and Grace* (Philadelphia: Fortress Press, 1972), 89, 99.

25. I think Barth is right to object that Lutheran Christology, with its overemphasis on the man Jesus, invites Ludwig Feuerbach's formula: "God becomes man, man becomes God." The Reformed *finitum non capax infiniti* disallows this. See Karl Barth, "An Introductory Essay," in Ludwig Feuerbach, *The Essence of Christianity* (New York: Harper Torchbooks, 1957), xxiii.

26. Michael A. Cowan notes that the spirit of bureaucracy and rational-instrumental planning poses a daunting challenge for liturgical celebration in our time. "Sacramental Moments: Appreciative Awareness in the Iron Cage," *Alternative Futures for Worship, Volume 1: General Introduction,* ed. Regis A. Duffy, O.F.M. (Collegeville, Minnesota: The Liturgical Press, 1987), 35, 46. See also Paul Tillich, *Theology of Culture* (New York: Oxford University Press, 1964), 53–60, and Langdon Gilkey, *Through the Tempest: Theological Voyages in a Pluralistic Culture* (Minneapolis: Fortress Press, 1991), 49–65. In his important discussion of religious language as symbolic language, Tillich refers to the debate over the Lord's Supper between Luther and Zwingli at Marburg in 1529, but he does not take into account Calvin's third position. I think that, in many respects, Tillich's understanding of symbol better accords with Calvin's eucharistic theology than with Luther's. Gilkey makes the important point that the divine works in and on us as creatures, and that much hangs on our awakening to our own role as symbols—in our lives, meanings, decisions, and hopes.

27. All that I have said here is informed by John E. Smith's understanding of media of disclosure. I agree with Smith that every experience of the reality of God is, at the same time, an experience of something else. See *Experience and God* (New York: Oxford University Press, 1968), 51–52, 68–98.

28. This is only to say in my own terms something that was especially well said by Paul Tillich in *Systematic Theology* (Chicago: University of Chicago Press, 1967), 3:102–6.

29. H. Richard Niebuhr, *H. Richard Niebuhr: Theology, History, and Culture,* ed. William Stacy Johnson (New Haven, Conn.: Yale University Press, 1996), 22. Much of what I say here is indebted to Niebuhr's discussion in his Cole Lecture entitled "Toward New Symbols."

30. In this sense, knowledge of God is always knowledge of something else at the same time. See Smith, *Experiential Religion,* 71.

31. Johanna W. H. van Wijk-Bos, *Reimagining God: The Case for Scriptural Diversity* (Louisville: Westminster John Knox, 1995), 99. Rosemary Radford Ruether points out that the exclusive use of male images can become idolatrous. See *Sexism and God-Talk: Toward a Feminist Theology* (Boston: Beacon Press, 1983), 66–68.

32. Much of what I say here is not unlike some points made by Karl Barth about the Word of God and witnesses to it. See *Church Dogmatics,* ed. G. W. Bromiley and T. F. Torrance (Edinburgh: T. & T. Clark, 1975), 1/1:88–124.

33. Of course, an appreciation for legitimate plurality should not exempt subtraditions from legitimate criticism. Philip Schaff suggested that more than a few doctrinal differences have roots in self-serving polemics. See *Philip Schaff: Historian and Ambassador of the Universal Church,* ed. Klaus Penzel (Macon, Ga.: Mercer University Press, 1991), 302–40. In *The Social Sources of Denominationalism* (New York: World Publishing Company, 1972), H. Richard Niebuhr pointed out that a good many denominational divisions have their roots in racial, ethnic, political, and economic interests that run contrary to the gospel. There is more than a little truth in what both Niebuhr and Schaff had to say.

34. John H. Hick, *A Christian Theology of the Religions: The Rainbow of Faiths* (Louisville: Westminster John Knox, 1995), 12–13. Robert McAfee Brown, *The Ecumenical Revolution: An Interpretation of the Catholic–Protestant Dialogue* (Garden City, N.Y.: Doubleday, 1967), 304–5 regards interreligious dialogue as an extension of ecumenical dialogue among Christians. It is a "wider dialogue with the world." See also Hick's comments about "the Christian superiority-complex" in *The Metaphor of God Incarnate: Christology in a Pluralistic Age* (Louisville: Westminster/John Knox, 1993), 80, 86–88.

35. John H. Hick's *Death and Eternal Life* (San Francisco: Harper & Row, 1976) counts as a rather subtle example of this. Although Hick admits a plurality of "mythic cultic substances" of the religions, he regards these substances as aspects of civilization which must be distinguished from "central affirmations concerning the nature of reality" (29). These affirmations are the theologies of the religions, and while they are "not identical," they make truth claims that may be synthesized. Hick's inquiry, although admittedly undertaken from a "christian" religious standpoint is not intended "primarily as a contribution to christian theology, but rather as a christian contribution to global or human theology" (27). His "tentative conclusion" is that the theologies of the religions do indeed "converge" and point toward "a common conception of human destiny" (34).

Hick's later work, *A Christian Theology of Religions: The Rainbow of Faiths* comes closer to the sort of ecumenical theology I have in mind. Here, he argues that the awareness of religious pluralism as well as inter-religious conversations offer good reasons why the traditional stance that Christianity is the only true religion is no longer workable. "An undogmatic Christianity, centered on the person and teachings of Jesus, is being heard again, alongside the teachings of Buddhism and of Hinduism and Islam and other traditions" (139).

36. I think a number of positions count as exclusionary in this sense. R. C. Sproul, John Gerstner, and Arthur Lindsay define apologetics as "the reasoned defense of the Christian religion" that "explains why Christians are Christians and why non-Christians should be Christians." They also devote a good deal of their book to criticizing Cornelius Van Til's presuppositional approach. They claim that Van Til is fideist. See *Classical Apologetics: A Rational Defense of the Christian Faith and Critique of Presuppositional Apologetics* (Grand Rapids, Mich.: Academie Books, Zondervan Publishing House, 1984), 16, 183–8. Van Til's work in apologetics remains worthy of attention, in part because it touches on the question of Christian subtraditions and their different theologies. "A Reformed method of apologetics must seek to vindicate the Reformed life and world view as Christianity come into its own." See *The Defense of the Faith* (Philadelphia: Presbyterian and Reformed Publishing Company, 1955), 113.

Mark M. Hanna, *Crucial Questions in Apologetics* (Grand Rapids, Mich.: Baker Book House, 1981), 107–9, also takes on presuppositionalism. Hanna claims that apologetics necessarily exposes "the fallacious assumptions and erroneous conclusions of the positions of others." However, it also explicates the nature of knowledge. Richard B. Cunningham develops an apologetics that advocates and defends Christianity but always also offers an invitation to the adherent of another world view to commit to Jesus Christ. *Christian Faith and Its Contemporary Rivals* (Nashville: Broadman Press, 1988), 203–4.

37. On difficulties that emerge when one tries to articulate generic concepts, see Wilfred Cantwell Smith, *Towards a World Theology: Faith and the Comparative History of Religion* (Philadelphia: Westminster Press, 1981), 180–94.

38. See David Tracy, *The Analogical Imagination: Christian Theology and the Culture of Pluralism* (New York: Crossroad Publishing Company, 1981), 450.

39. Gordon D. Kaufman suggests that everyday conversations among equals and friends can furnish a helpful model for interreligious dialogues, and the conversations I have in mind here are not entirely unlike the sort he endorses. "Each participant in the conversation posits the others as substantive contributors in this collective pursuit of (religious) truth, and thus is open in principle to collaboration with those others—instead of these several voices each presuming it is capable of expressing (by itself) what needs to be said." *God-Mystery-Diversity: Christian Theology in a Pluralistic World* (Minneapolis: Fortress Press, 1996), 201.

6. Engaging Culture

1. John Calvin, *The Second Epistle of Paul the Apostle to the Corinthians and the Epistles to Timothy, Titus, and Philemon,* trans. T. A. Small (Grand Rapids, Mich.: Eerdmans, 1964), 363–64. The statement I have in mind is one Calvin makes in commentary on Titus 1:12.

2. See, for example, Wade Clark Roof and William McKinney, *American Mainline Religion: Its Changing Shape and Future* (New Brunswick, N.J.: Rutgers University Press, 1987); Robert Wuthnow, *The Restructuring of American Religion: Society and Faith Since World War II* (Princeton, N.J.: Princeton University Press, 1988).

3. Friedrich Schleiermacher, *The Christian Faith,* ed. H. R. Mackintosh and J. S. Stewart (Philadelphia: Fortress Press, 1976), 200–219.

4. Abraham Kuyper, *Calvinism* (New York: Fleming H. Revell Company, n.d.), 99.

5. H. Richard Niebuhr, *The Responsible Self: An Essay in Christian Moral Philosophy* (New York: Harper & Row, 1963), 108–26.

6. John Calvin, *Institutes of the Christian Religion,* trans. Ford Lewis Battles, ed. John T. McNeill (Philadelphia: Westminster Press, 1960), I, xiv, 21; xv, 4.

7. Jonathan Edwards, "Original Sin," *The Works of Jonathan Edwards* (Carlisle, Pa.: Banner of Truth, 1974), 1:149–51.

8. Calvin, *Institutes,* II, ii, 12–18. Edwards, *Works,* 1:122–39. This is evidence of God's mercy and continuing care, or the common grace of God in distinction from saving grace.

9. Calvin, *Institutes,* III, iii, 16; xiv, 5.

10. Horace Bushnell, *The New Life* (London: Richard D. Dickinson, 1885), 69.

11. Karl Barth, *The German Church Conflict* (Richmond, Va.: John Knox Press, 1965), 72.

12. See chapter 1, "Leadership-Speak in Contemporary Society."

13. For a more detailed account see my chapter on "The Church In, With, Against, and For the World" in *Reforming Protestantism: Christian Commitment in Today's World* (Louisville: Westminster John Knox, 1995), 93–116.

14. "The Confession of 1967," in *The Constitution of the Presbyterian Church (U.S.A.): Part I, Book of Confessions* (Louisville: Office of the General Assembly, 1994), 9.31 (p. 265).

7. The Ministry of Reconciliation

1. Particularly in America, the literature on ministerial leadership is immense and very uneven. H. Richard Niebuhr noted in 1956 that there was little agreement as to what ministry is or should be. *The Purpose of the Church and Its Ministry* (New York: Harper & Row, 1957), 51. Current studies and handbooks treat everything from spiritual authority, empowering others, and teamwork, to financial planning and how to manage church boards. Charles Tidwell begins his book on *Church Administration: Effective Leadership for Ministry* (Nashville: Broadman Press, 1985) by saying that "Church administration has come of age. Since 1950, more attention has been focused on church administration than perhaps all the prior years of church history" (p. 11). Certainly, there is little reason to doubt this statement in 1999. An interesting and informative contribution to the literature is *The Responsibility People: Eighteen Senior Leaders of Protestant Churches and National Ecumenical Agencies Reflect on Church Leadership,* ed. William McKinney (Grand Rapids, Mich.: Eerdmans, 1994).

2. Richard Baxter, *Gildas Salvianus. The Reformed Pastor* in *The Practical Works of Richard Baxter* (Ligonier, Penn.: Soli Deo Gloria Publications, 1990–91), vol. IV, 367. Baxter begins by citing Acts 20:28, which he has as follows. "Take heed therefore unto yourselves, and to all the flock, over which the Holy Ghost hath made you overseers, to feed the church of God, which he hath purchased with his own blood."

3. The Confession of 1967 of the Presbyterian Church (U.S.A.) is built around the theme of reconciliation, and it says that "God's reconciling work in Jesus Christ and the mission of reconciliation to which he has called his church are the heart of the gospel in any age." *The Constitution of the Presbyterian Church (U.S.A.), Part I: The Book of Confessions* (Louisville: The Office of the General Assembly, 1994), 9.06 (p. 262). Hereafter cited as BOC, 9.06 (p. 262).

4. This helps to explain its power, although in the Bible we find something approaching a theology of reconciliation only in the Pauline corpus, and although the theme of reconciliation occurs only sporadically even in Paul. See *Encyclopedia of Biblical Theology: The Complete Sacramentum Verbi,* ed. Johannes B. Bauer (New York: Crossroad, 1981), 730–38.

5. The nineteenth-century liberal theologian Albrecht Ritschl had something like this in mind when he claimed that "sin is the negative presupposition of reconciliation." *The Christian Doctrine of Justification and Reconciliation: The Positive Development of the Doctrine,* ed. H. R. Mackintosh and A. B. Macaulay (Clifton, N.J.: Reference Book Publishers, 1966), 327.

6. Karl Barth, *Church Dogmatics,* trans. G. W. Bromiley and T. F. Torrance (Edinburgh: T. &. T. Clark, 1956), 4/1:22.

7. H. Richard Niebuhr, *The Responsible Self: An Essay in Christian Moral Philosophy* (New York: Harper & Row, 1963), 44. Niebuhr is correct, I think, to mention the reconciliation of people not only to God and to one another, but also to the world. Indeed, Colossians 1:19–22 points to the universal scope and cosmic dimensions of reconciliation in a way that should keep us from limiting the symbol to God and persons alone.

8. John Calvin, *The Second Epistle of Paul the Apostle to the Corinthians and the Epistles to Timothy,* trans. T. A. Small, ed. David W. Torrance and Thomas F. Torrance

(Grand Rapids, Mich.: Eerdmans, 1964), 78. On God going-out from Godself as Father, Son, and Spirit, see chapter 3 above, "The Sense the Trinity Makes."

9. I comment in more detail on sin, fragmentation, and conflict in chapter 6, "Engaging Culture," and also in *Reforming Protestantism: Christian Commitment in Today's World* (Louisville: Westminster John Knox, 1995), 66–73.

10. I discuss this is more detail in *Reforming Protestantism,* 104–8.

11. The Corinthians even managed to turn the eucharistic meal into an occasion for division. In this, too, they anticipated us. See Peter Lampe, "The Corinthian Eucharistic Dinner Party: Exegesis of a Cultural Context," *Affirmation* 4, no. 2 (fall 1991): 1–15.

12. The Confession of 1967 of the Presbyterian Church (U.S.A.) notes that the scriptures describe this mystery in various ways. "It is called the sacrifice of a lamb, a shepherd's life given for his sheep, atonement by a priest; again, it is ransom of a slave, payment of a debt, vicarious satisfaction of a legal penalty, and victory over the powers of evil. These are expressions of a truth which remains beyond the reach of all theory in the depths of God's love for man." BOC, 9.09 (p. 262). I present my own approach to the atonement in *Jesus Christ and Christian Vision* (Louisville: Westminster John Knox, 1995), 85–93.

13. The words of invitation are from *The Book of Common Worship* (Louisville: Westminster/John Knox, 1993), 68, and they pick up words and themes from Luke 13:29. The Confession of 1967 of the Presbyterian Church (U.S.A.) regards the Lord's Supper as "a celebration of the reconciliation of men with God and one another" as well as a "foretaste of the kingdom." BOC, 9.52 (p. 270). Of course, in a world where Christians themselves do not enjoy full communion with one another, the Supper points toward a reality that may also subvert our own divisive eucharistic and ecclesiastical practices.

14. I offer a preliminary definition of the church in *Reforming Protestantism,* 94–100.

15. This is H. Richard Niebuhr's specification of the purpose of the church in *The Purpose of the Church and Its Ministry,* 31.

16. *A Testament of Hope: The Essential Writings of Martin Luther King, Jr.,* ed. James Melvin Washington (San Francisco: Harper & Row, 1986), 12, 87.

17. BOC, 9.01 (p. 261).

18. See, for example, Martin Luther King Jr.'s comment that, despite shortcomings, Walter Rauschenbusch and the social gospel "gave to American Protestantism a sense of social responsibility that it should never lose." *A Testament of Hope,* 37.

General Index

Scripture Index